TANKMASTER

An essential guide to choosing your

COLD WATER

AQUARIUM FISH

NICK FLETCHER

BARRON'S

Author

Nick Fletcher is a former editor of *Practical Fishkeeping* and still regularly contributes articles to this and other aquatic publications. His interest in tropical and cold water fish stems from his lifelong hobby of fishing, which resulted in tanks containing several oddities, including pike. Nowadays, he prefers keeping fish to catching them, and is actively involved in koi circles at local and national levels. Instead of a lawn he has a koi pond.

First published in 2000 by Interpet Publishing under the title *An Essential Guide to Choosing Your Coldwater Aquarium Fish.* © Copyright 2000 by Interpet Publishing. All rights reserved. First edition for the United States and Canada published in 2000 by Barron's Educational Series, Inc.

All inquiries should be addressed to:
Barron's Educational Series, Inc., 250 Wireless Boulevard, Hauppauge, New York 11788
http://www.barronseduc.com

International Standard Book Number 0-7641-5273-4
Library of Congress Catalog Card Number 00-91887

Printed in China
9 8 7 6 5 4 3 2 1

Below: Comets are among the most streamlined of goldfish varieties. Their long tails give them speed as well as elegance. These sarasa comets display a handsome combination of red and white markings.

Contents

These are ryukin, one of many deep-bodied, long-finned goldfish varieties.

The world's most popular pet

The goldfish is the world's most popular pet, and many people setting up their first cold water aquarium find that this readily available favorite, with so many varieties to choose from, satisfies all their needs. Naturally, this book will cover a number of the most popular fancy goldfish, beginning with the least demanding and moving on to some exotic types that require more specialized care. But the story does not end there. Visiting your local aquarium store, you will probably have seen many other cold water fish and wondered if they would be right for you. This guide will give you the answers, plus a varied selection of suitable species from all over the world.

While goldfish can live happily within a wide temperature range, many other so-called "cold water" species cannot. This is especially true of those that are not commercially farmed for the aquarium trade. Wild-caught fish come from widely differing habitats, and to keep them successfully you must replicate the natural conditions as closely as possible. For some, this might even mean installing a heater in the tank. This does not mean approaching tropical temperatures, but a section of the book will nevertheless be devoted to fish that prefer a slightly warm tank.

Finally, for the adventurous fishkeeper, we look at some species with the potential to grow really big. These clearly require spacious accommodation, and in many cases need to be kept alone, or only with others of their own kind and of equal size. Such "tankbusters" can develop real personalities and become true family pets.

Bear in mind that many cold water aquarium species originate from Europe and the United States. Accidental transfer or deliberate introduction of these fish into waters where they do not naturally belong can endanger the native fish, and laws are in place to prevent this from happening. Check your local regulations if you are in doubt.

There are also legal restrictions governing what fish you can and cannot keep, and these will vary from country to country and from state to state, so check out the local regulations before committing yourself.

Always obtain permission to collect your own fish, and never take more than you need. Above all, ensure that the tank you are providing for them back home meets all their requirements, and that feeding will not be a problem. As you will see, some of the species described in this book will eat only live foods, which can be hard to provide all year round.

Throughout this book we mention the names of fins and other parts of the body. The photographs of a typical goldfish (a plant-eater) and a spotted gar (a carnivore) show that although fish vary greatly in appearance, all have features in common. Only where man has intervened to breed goldfish selectively do we find great variations in body shape, color, finnage, and scalation within a single species.

Fins and what they do

The fins of all the species described in this book fall into two categories: single and paired. Used together, they stabilize the fish, help it swim through the water and enable it to make fine maneuvers when feeding, breeding, or avoiding predators.

Single fins include the dorsal (top) fin, caudal (tail) fin, and the anal fin, which starts behind the fish's vent. Some fish, notably members of the salmon family, have an additional fatty adipose fin behind the dorsal. Its function is not known. The paired fins are the pectoral and ventral (or pelvic) fins.

The fins and their position on the body of a fish are useful pointers to its lifestyle. A classically "fish-shaped" fish, such as a minnow, dace, or common goldfish, is adapted to cope with most situations without being specialized. It spends most of its time swimming calmly along, occasionally accelerating to chase prey or avoid capture. On the other hand, the dorsal and anal fins of a pike or gar are set far back toward its tail. This "dragster rig" is ideal for making short bursts of speed, but is not designed for sustained fast swimming. If the pike does not catch its meal at the first lunge, it will not pursue it. It is

The fins of a typical fish

This common goldfish has the "standard" arrangement of fins found in most of the fish featured in this book.

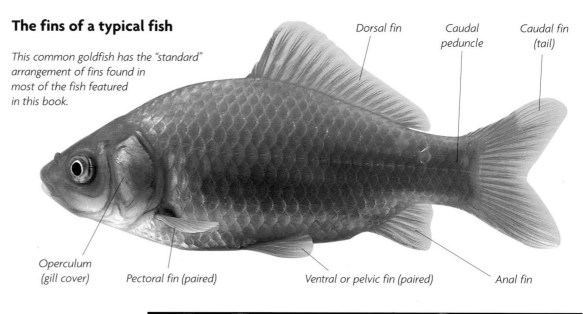

Dorsal fin

Caudal peduncle

Caudal fin (tail)

Operculum (gill cover)

Pectoral fin (paired)

Ventral or pelvic fin (paired)

Anal fin

Right: Spotted gar (Lepisosteus oculatus) in a public aquarium. The dorsal and anal fins are close by the tail, forming a dragster-style propulsion unit for speed from a standing start.

not widely known that while fins help provide initial thrust, it is the sinuous S-shaped movements of a fish's body that keep it moving through the water.

Other clues to lifestyle

Looking at the mouth, eyes, and body shape of a fish broadens our understanding of how it lives, and thus helps us to replicate ideal conditions in the aquarium. For example, a protrusible mouth equipped with barbels (feelers) suggests a fish that feeds on or near the bottom. Most of the carp family, however, are omnivorous, meaning they eat a wide variety of plant matter and small aquatic life forms. These fish have no teeth in the mouth, but specialized pharyngeal teeth set farther back in the throat, designed to crush up food items before they

Below: Proudly displaying its moustache of four pairs of barbels, this weather loach (Misgurnus anguillicaudatus) *is perfectly designed for locating food items in the substrate.*

Right: This American Perca flavescens (a member of the perch family) clearly shows the lateral line along its flank. This is a sensory organ unique to fish, and performs several functions simultaneously, including detecting vibrations in the water.

are passed down to the gut. Contrast these with the rows of backward-facing, pointed teeth belonging to the pike. They have one function alone: to hook into and hold prey before it is swallowed whole. Common sense alone will tell you not to keep a pike with your goldfish!

Open-water swimmers have relatively large eyes to help them locate food by sight and to avoid predators. Binocular vision is most well developed in the carnivorous species. Small eyes are more characteristic of fish that spend time on or near the bottom, hidden under rocks or in the mud. The weather loach *(Misgurnus anguillicaudatus)* has tiny eyes, but it locates food with the aid of sensitive barbels that correspond to our senses of touch and taste. A fish from fast-flowing water (a good example is the barbel, *Barbus barbus*) tends to have a flattened belly and a wedge-shaped head profile, so that the current pushes it down onto the substrate where it feeds.

There is one fish sensory organ – the lateral line – with no human equivalent. This line of sensory organs running along each side of the fish picks up vibrations in the water and alerts the fish to nearby obstacles, danger, or the presence of food. Thanks to this organ, even fish that have lost one or both eyes can still get by in an aquarium.

Natural habitat

Other than those mass-produced on farms, cold water fish are found in widely diverse habitats around the world, where water temperature and chemistry, the level of dissolved oxygen, and the speed of the current all differ greatly. Some species are best suited to cool, fast-flowing mountain streams, others to lakes and ponds. Shallow, still waters are prone to rapid heating and cooling; rivers can alternate between winter melt waters or summer doldrums, when the flow is reduced to a trickle. All these habitats have fish populations that are adaptable to a degree (and can even survive some environmental pollution). But our duty is to provide our captive fish with the best possible aquarium environment; their mere survival is not good enough.

Catching fish from the wild

Collecting your own specimens of small native fish can be great fun and very satisfying. The easiest species to catch are those that live under stones in shallow, fast-flowing streams, such as bullheads and loaches. Wade gently into the water and walk up the current until you find a likely looking stone. Position a fine-meshed hand net on the downstream side of this and lift the stone gently. Anything living beneath will dart out and be caught in the mesh. Some fish have spines on their fins or gill covers. Disentangle these gently, in order not to harm the captives. For deeper, slower water you can make a trap from a plastic bottle. Remove the cap, cut off the neck and invert it inside the bottle to form an inner cone. Secure this with silicone sealant. Make a sling from cord tied around the bottle and attach a longer piece of cord to this so that you can retrieve the trap later on. Bait with a cube of frozen bloodworm, a few chopped worms, or a piece of bread. A fragment of red flannel may attract male sticklebacks in the breeding season; they see it as a territorial rival. Weight the trap with a stone and lower it into the water so that it fills completely. Then maneuver it so that the cone-shaped end faces upstream. Lured by the bait, fish will enter the trap and be unable to get out again through the narrow cone.

Equipment you will need

Plastic bucket to hold immediate captures.
Plastic bags and rubber bands for transporting fish home.
A cooler, so that the fish do not overheat on the journey.
Two or three sizes of fine-meshed net.
Bottle trap. (See the construction details shown opposite.)

Do's and don'ts

Do not leave the trap unattended for too long. If you are going to catch anything, an hour should be quite sufficient.
Do not collect fish without permission, and unless you have a suitable tank already set up for them.
Do not take more specimens than you need.
Do not overcrowd your transit bags.
Do not mix species in transit, or large fish with small.
Do not collect endangered or prohibited species.
Do replace all stones and rocks as you found them.
Do check that you are not bringing home "undesirables" such as carnivorous aquatic insects.
Do get back home without delay.

A simple bottle trap

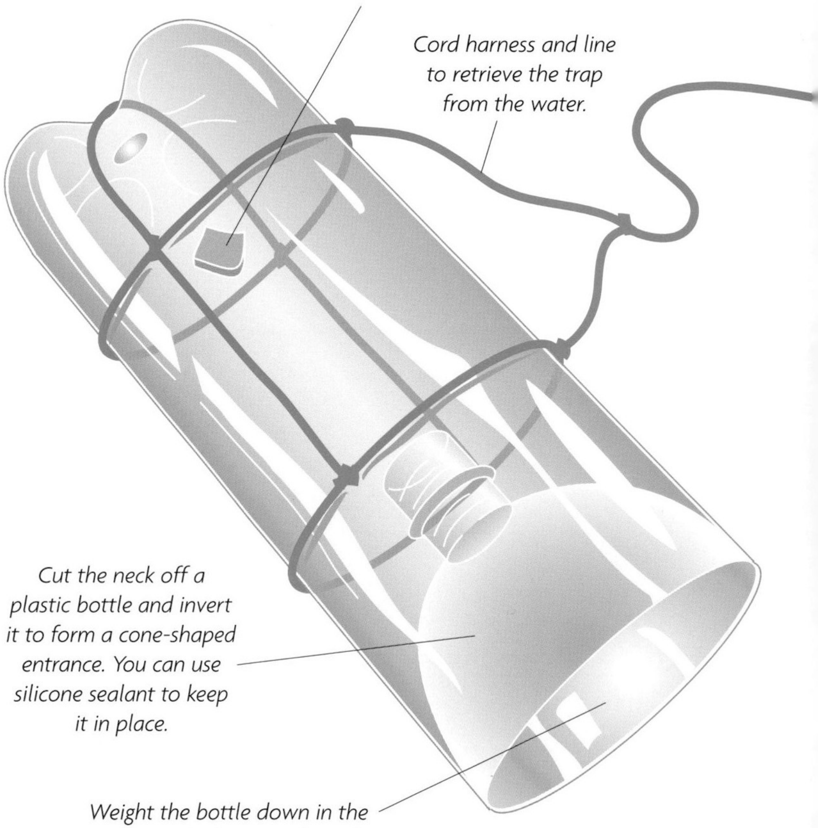

Bait the trap with bread, chopped worms, or a frozen bloodworm cube.

Cord harness and line to retrieve the trap from the water.

Cut the neck off a plastic bottle and invert it to form a cone-shaped entrance. You can use silicone sealant to keep it in place.

Weight the bottle down in the water with the cone-shaped end facing upstream.

Above: *An English chalkstream in early summer. Clean, fairly shallow habitats like this are ideal fish-collecting grounds – but only if you have the permission of the river owner. Do not collect protected fish species.*

How the information panels work throughout the book

The basic requirements for keeping each species are given in an easy-to-read panel, such as the example below (this is for the White Cloud Mountain minnow). Breeding details, if available, are given in a separate text block.

Water quality
This highlights the range of water conditions required by each fish.

Temperature
This gives the range within which the fish lives.

Food
Advice on the range of foods each fish will accept. Wherever possible, these items are commonly available.

Minimum number
Some fish require to be kept in groups, others singly.

Minimum tank size
This is the smallest aquarium you should consider for each species. Tanks are available in a range of standard sizes, such as 60x30x30 cm (24x12x12 in) and 90x30x38 cm (36x12x15 in).

Tank region
Some fish swim at all levels, others inhabit particular zones (the top or the surface) for most of the time. If you mix species in the same tank, this information will help you achieve a visually balanced setup.

▶ *Ideal conditions*

Water: Neutral, soft to slightly hard.
Temperature: 18–23°C (64–73°F).
Food: Small live or frozen aquatic invertebrates, such as daphnia, mosquito larvae, and bloodworm. Flake foods. Offer a varied diet.
Minimum number in the aquarium: 6.
Minimum tank size: 45 cm (18 in).
Tank region: Middle to top.

▶ *Breeding*

The male courts his chosen female, spreading his fins and swimming around her until the pair come together and swim over some fine-leaved plants, shedding eggs and milt (sperm). The fertilized eggs hatch after 36 hours and the fry need fine live foods. These fish are very easy to breed in cool conditions, so many fishkeepers put them outside during the warm summer months, when the fish breed readily in plant-filled ponds and tubs.

Any aquarium holding more than one species of fish will involve compromise. This is especially true of a tropical community tank, where fish from all over the globe are held under one set of conditions that is inevitably less than ideal for each individual.

Cold water tanks do not pose quite the same problem. They are either single species setups – typically fancy goldfish – or else the mix (and hence the risk of getting it wrong) is greatly reduced. However, it is still important to know what size of tank suits each fish and which zone of the water – top, middle, or bottom – it prefers. And it is vital to avoid potentially disastrous combinations of species. This goes well beyond the classic error of mixing predator with prey. Here are some general points to consider to ensure that your fish get along together and are content.

The balance of fish in the aquarium

For each species, we suggest a minimum number that you should keep in the smallest recommended aquarium. Sometimes the minimum is also the maximum – one! This holds true for predatory fish – those that would fight even with their own kind – or specimens that grow so large that there is room in the tank for only a single individual. Otherwise, if fish can be accurately sexed, always buy a pair. If this proves impossible, obtaining six youngsters will give you a better than 90% chance of having males and females. Six is also the minimum number to consider for schooling species, which not only look better in a group, but behave as they would in the wild. Schooling (a common characteristic of cyprinids) offers protection from predators and improved chances of finding food and a mate.

Size does matter

Mixing large and small fish in the same tank is not a good idea. In the wild, even members of the carp family happily devour their own fry, and a big goldfish will do the same to any tankmate that will fit into its mouth.

The effects of antagonistic behavior are most evident when there is a considerable size difference between the fish concerned. But sometimes the very presence of a large fish, however peaceful, will intimidate smaller tankmates.

Fancy goldfish are so diverse that often one variety will bully or harass another, irrespective of size. Usually it is the faster-swimming types, closest in shape to the wild ancestor, that pick on goldfish with exaggerated finnage. It is possible that a shubunkin sees a veiltail, not as another goldfish, but as an entirely different species!

Many cold water fish will eventually outgrow their tanks and need rehousing. The rate of growth in goldfish is genetically determined, and some individuals will shoot ahead of the rest for no obvious reason. It is a myth that large cold water species will not attain full size in an aquarium. With the proper diet, good filtration, and regular water changes they will keep on growing, sometimes to the point where they cannot turn around. This is obviously something to avoid, but never be tempted to release these mature fish back into the wild.

Territorial squabbles

Fish such as the male stickleback, which exercises brood care, establish defended "territories" at

Left: *The pike (Esox lucius) is an obvious predator, and few fishkeepers would make the basic mistake of housing it with smaller fish, even of its own species. But finding the right mix is not always that clear-cut.*

spawning time. These are quite large and impossible to duplicate in the average aquarium. Every other tank occupant is always within the stickleback's "personal space" and will be attacked, whatever its size. This is good enough reason to give all species with the potential to breed a tank to themselves.

Another form of territoriality is seen when a newcomer is introduced to several fish that have grown up together. The "intruder" disrupts the habits and movement patterns of the rest and may well be attacked and killed by otherwise peaceable tankmates. A way of tackling this problem is to rearrange the decor by moving around rocks, bogwood, or plastic plants, so that every fish has to start from scratch in staking its claim. Just as in a tropical tank, the chances of territorial disputes are reduced if all three layers of the water have their specific occupants.

How many fish to a tank?
The density of fish population for a tank of a given size is determined by its surface area. The cooler the water, the less efficient biofiltration becomes, so as a rule of thumb, a cold water tank will support only half the numbers of an equivalent tropical setup. For a filtered tank, allow 150 sq cm (24 sq in) of surface area per 2.5 cm (1 in) body length, not including tails. A tank measuring 60x30 cm (24x12 in) has a surface area of 1800 sq cm (288 sq in) and will hold about 30 cm (12 in) of cold water fish. The more efficient the filtration and the higher the water temperature, the more fish you can stock, always assuming they are compatible! Be cautious if your fish are very large and bulky. In this case it is best to understock rather than overstock the tank, as big fish produce more organic waste length for length than small ones, and have a higher oxygen requirement.

Right: A school of mosquitofish (Gambusia affinis) in a single-species aquarium. Adhere to the basic stocking guidelines below, remembering that quality of filtration and frequency of water changes are just as important as tank size for long-term success.

This 60x30 cm (24x12 in) tank contains two fish, each measuring 15 cm (6 in) long, which together add up to the maximum carrying capacity of 30 cm (12 in) of fish body length.

The same 60x30 cm (24x12 in) tank could house six fish, each measuring 5 cm (2 in) long, which together add up to the maximum carrying capacity of 30 cm (12 in) of fish body length.

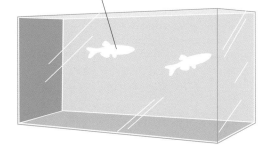

It is impossible to keep fish without maintaining the right water conditions. Some of these parameters, such as temperature and pH, need to vary according to species. Others apply to every single one; aim for zero ammonia and nitrite readings at all times, for example (see the panel on page 15).

The pH and hardness of aquarium water

Wherever possible, choose fish that will thrive in your local water supply, rather than try to alter the water chemistry to suit the fish. The most important considerations are pH (the degree of acidity or alkalinity of the water) and hardness (the amount of dissolved calcium or magnesium salts present). Both are difficult to alter without expensive chemical regulators, and even then, you cannot guarantee long-term stability. Remember that your choice of substrate can affect water hardness.

Most of the species described in this book are happy with a pH value between 6.5 and 7.5, either side of the neutral reading of pH 7.0, and slightly soft to moderately hard water.

The pH scale explained

The term "pH" is short for "potential Hydrogen" and reflects the balance between positively charged hydrogen ions (H^+) and negatively charged hydroxyl ions (OH^-) in the water. The more hydrogen ions present, the more acidic the water, and the more hydroxyl ions, the more alkaline it becomes. When there is an equal balance, the water is said to be neutral (pH 7.0). Although the pH scale runs from pH 0 (extremely acidic) to pH 14 (extremely alkaline), fish cannot survive these extremes, which rarely occur in nature. The pH scale is logarithmic; in other words, water at pH 9.0 is 10 times more alkaline than

at pH 8.0. To monitor the pH of your aquarium, use liquid or tablet test kits, paper strips (which give a color comparison indication), or an electronic meter for an accurate digital readout.

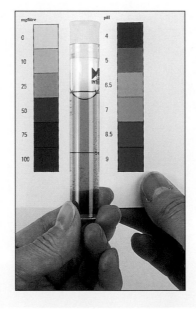

Right: You can check the pH reading of your water with the simple test shown here. Add a tablet to the water sample, shake the tube well and compare the color change to a printed chart.

Water temperature

Even in a cold water aquarium it is important to maintain a stable temperature. In a room that is centrally heated 24 hours a day this can be achieved without using a heater/thermostat. But if, for example, your tank is located in a place where the air temperature fluctuates significantly, an aquarium heater will even out the peaks and troughs. That said, some cold water fish are triggered into spawning by a seasonal rise or fall in temperature – another use for this piece of equipment.

If your aquarium contains more than one species, the water temperature can be adjusted to suit them all, even if the upper and lower extremes for each differ by a few degrees. Fancy goldfish have a very wide temperature tolerance of about 10–26°C (50–79°F), so that a number of tankmates can be fitted around them. For example, you could keep weather loach (preferred range 10–15°C/50–59°F), shiners (15–24°C/59–75°F) and gudgeon (10–18°C/50–64°F) with fancy goldfish, setting the heater to 15°C (59°F). That would be the upper limit for the loach, the lower limit for the shiner, midway in the gudgeon's temperature range, and perfectly acceptable for the goldfish, too.

Oxygen levels

All fish need oxygen to live, which they extract through their gills. If surface agitation is provided by means of an air pump or the return from a power filter, this will allow oxygen to enter the water and carbon dioxide to leave it. Cool water holds more dissolved oxygen than warm, so cold water aquariums are unlikely to suffer a shortage. However, it is a still good idea to have a spare air pump to boost aeration if this ever becomes necessary.

Regular maintenance

Regularly attending to simple maintenance tasks and ensuring good water quality will reduce the risk of disease and prolong the lives of your fish.

During daily feeding, you will get the chance to find out if anything is amiss. Are all the fish coming up eagerly for food or is one hanging back and looking miserable? (Do not overfeed; one or two small meals, eaten within 5–10 minutes, are quite sufficient. Remove uneaten food after that time, except for "green" items, such as lettuce or cucumber, which can be replenished daily.)

Check the water temperature first thing every day. If a heater is fitted, it could have stuck in the "on" position and raised it to a dangerously high level. Also ensure that the flow rate through your filter has not reduced. If it has, the media will need cleaning.

Every week or two, conduct a 10–20% partial water change, siphoning out old water and replacing it with fresh, conditioned tapwater at the correct temperature. If you have an undergravel filter, remove old water using a gravel cleaner, which pulls dirt from the substrate and slows down the rate of clogging. Rinse the media inside internal and external power filters in rotation and replace "disposable" material, such as dirty filter floss.

You will soon work out your own maintenance schedule, based on the size and type of aquarium and the species and numbers of fish you keep. The key word is "regular." Keeping a log is the best way to make sure that everything is done when it should be, and that equipment is checked over, serviced, or replaced at the recommended intervals.

Above: Flaked food is the ideal staple diet for most cold water fish, but you should vary this with frozen, freeze-dried, or live food items. How would you like pizza every day?

Measuring water hardness

In the fish profiles you will see terms such as "slightly soft" or "moderately hard" to describe the degree of water hardness that best suits each species in the aquarium. There are several units to measure this parameter. The one most widely used is degrees of hardness (°dH). The following table shows how that scale compares to our general descriptions and to another commonly used scale, that of milligrams of calcium carbonate ($CaCO_3$) per liter of water, which equates to parts per million (ppm).

Description	°dH	Mg/liter (ppm) $CaCO_3$
Soft	0–3	0–50
Slightly soft	3–6	50–100
Slightly hard	6–12	100–200
Moderately hard	12–18	200–300
Hard	18–25	300–450
Very hard	25+	450+

New tank syndrome

The most common health pitfall – and one that occurs in the early stages of keeping an aquarium – arises from being in too much of a hurry to stock it with fish. This "new tank syndrome" is more accurately known as ammonia or nitrite poisoning and can be avoided by frequent water testing and carrying out partial water changes. Other problems develop more slowly. Even when the aquarium is established, forgetting water changes can lead to a build-up of nitrate which, although not very toxic, will stress the fish and lower their resistance to disease.

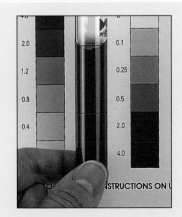

Left: Testing the water for nitrite level is a vital part of routine maintenance. This test involves adding a tablet to a sample of tank water in a tube, shaking it vigorously and comparing the color change to a printed chart. Here, the nitrite level is very high; it should be colorless.

If you start with healthy fish and maintain them properly, disease should not be a major problem. The most common ailments – fungus and white spot – are easy to treat with remedies off the shelf, but be sure to make the correct diagnosis; otherwise, treatment can do more harm than good. If fish are looking off-color, a water change is often all they need. Bacterial infections are more difficult to treat, so never buy fish showing lesions, ulcers, reddening of the fins, or a fungus-like growth around the lips.

Here, we look at a range of possible health problems and how to tackle them.

Fungus (dermatomycosis)

Seen as cotton wool-like growths on body and fins, fungus invades any breaches in the fish's mucus coat at sites of damage caused by injury, parasite attack, or abrupt changes in water chemistry. It can be triggered by a fish rubbing itself against a rough

object or being bullied by tankmates – the cause as well as the obvious effects of fungus must always be addressed. Minor cases can be treated topically by dabbing on a medicinal or commercial fungicide at the site of infection, but for more severe outbreaks, the whole tank will need medicating. Treatment is much more difficult when the fungus has invaded the body tissues. Do not confuse it with "mouth fungus," which looks similar but is a bacterial problem.

White spot (ichthyophthiriasis)

This is an easy condition to treat if caught early, but left untreated it will wipe out a tank in no time. The visible white pinhead-sized "spots" on the body and fins are only one stage in the life cycle of the ciliate parasite *Ichthyophthirius multifiliis*. They break out from under the skin to form cysts that fall to the bottom of the tank. These break open and release thousands of free-swimming forms that seek out a

fresh fish host, and it is at this stage that white spot is most susceptible to medication. The life cycle speeds up with rising water temperature, so the warmer the aquarium, the shorter the treatment period needed to eliminate all stages of the parasite.

Swimbladder problems

Affected fish find difficulty in maintaining their position in the water – they may swim at odd angles, or even bob to the surface and go belly-up before fighting to restore their balance. The condition most

Left: This carp is showing classic symptoms of white spot, where the parasites have embedded themselves in skin and fin tissue. Treat the whole tank with an off-the-shelf remedy for a complete cure.

Right: A pearlscale goldfish with an obvious swimbladder problem. Sometimes affected fish bob to the surface of the aquarium, but are just as likely to go head-down, unable to swim on an even keel.

commonly arises in short-bodied fancy goldfish, whose swimbladder is distorted. Sometimes feeding laxative foods such as daphnia, or warming the water, will help, but usually swimbladder problems are chronic. It is up to you to decide whether the fish's quality of life is being seriously affected, and if so, it is probably best to dispose of it humanely.

Dropsy

Like fungus, dropsy is not a primary ailment but a symptom of other things wrong with the fish. The body swells, scales stick out so that the fish resembles a pine cone, and the eyes protrude. This fluid imbalance can be brought about by an internal

Above: A fish louse (Argulus) *near the tail of a goldfish. Remove visible parasites manually, and watch for free-swimmers that may attach themselves later.*

bacterial infection, kidney failure, or the effects of a tumor, and in most instances any treatment given is ineffective. Mild cases may respond to medication with salt and a bactericide – isolate the affected fish in a hospital tank.

Ulcers

Red marks and open sores on the belly and sides are caused by *Aeromonas* bacteria. The disease is triggered by poor tank hygiene or the introduction of unquarantined fish. Minor cases may respond to small, frequent water changes and improved tank maintenance, and both topical and general treatment with a mild bactericide can be tried. For lesions that originate internally and then break out, antibiotic injections are the only answer – seek expert advice.

Finrot

Another problem associated with poorly maintained tanks, bacterial finrot is first seen as an erosion of the soft membranes between the fin rays, which may become red and inflamed. A water change and filter overhaul will often cure the problem if caught early, otherwise, the disease may spread to the body of the fish. Try topical treatment if only one fish is affected, or else medicate the whole tank with a bactericide. Keep a check on water quality, which may be affected by the medication.

Visible external parasites

Fish lice, leeches, and anchor worm sometimes come in on imported fishes and can usually be spotted at the time of purchase. Treatment in an aquarium is much easier than in a pond and consists of removing the parasites with tweezers and swabbing the wound sites with a bactericide. You can also treat the water with medication. Fish lice (*Argulus*) can swim away

Disposing of fish humanely

If a sick fish is beyond saving, the best thing is to dispose of it humanely. If you can bring yourself to do it, the quickest method is to sever the spinal cord behind the head with a sharp knife; alternatively, obtain the fish anesthetic MS222 from a veterinarian or pharmacist and leave the patient in a solution of this for several hours. Never flush a fish down the toilet, throw it on the floor, or place it alive in the freezer. Freezing first affects the capillary blood vessels just under the skin, causing the fish great pain before it loses consciousness.

from their host and return later, so check the fish at intervals to ensure that all have been dealt with successfully.

Split fins

Minor splits in fins, resulting from transit damage or squabbling between fish, will usually heal without intervention. If one fish is a constant aggressor, remove it to prevent the problem from recurring. Splits that completely divide the tail or go down to the fin root may become infected with fungus or bacteria – keep an eye on the site and treat appropriately.

Unexplained deaths

If one fish dies in an otherwise healthy tank, do not rule out old age. Goldfish can live for 10 years or more, but smaller cold water species such as White Cloud Mountain minnows will do well to last half that time. Generally you will see a fish slowly go down in condition before it dies, and you may feel that this is the time to intervene with humane disposal (see the panel on this page).

Goldfish varieties

Goldfish – red-scaled variants of an Oriental crucian carp – were first mentioned by the Chinese in the second century A.D. But only during the Ming Dynasty (1368–644) did they become popular as pets. As general interest in them grew, so did the selective breeding of mutations, which gave rise to the many, often bizarre, varieties we know today.

Exports of goldfish reached Japan (where they are known as "wakin") at the dawn of the sixteenth century. The first European goldfish were bred in 1728 in Amsterdam, but it was not until 1794 that we can be sure they reached the United Kingdom. Their arrival in the United States was delayed until 1852. While China and Japan can lay claim to developing most types of fancy goldfish, a few originated in the UK and the US. The comet, for example, is an American variety, while the London and Bristol shubunkins owe their names to the English cities where they were first bred.

All goldfish are members of the carp family (Cyprinidae), and differ from the common carp (the ancestral koi) in having no barbels. The scientific name *(Carassius auratus)* applies right across the board, even though the appearance of some varieties has changed almost beyond recognition from the wild fish.

Right: *This young common goldfish is showing black markings on the head and in the fins – these will almost certainly disappear as it gets older.*

Body shape and fins

Fancy goldfish are an incredibly diverse group. Body shape can vary from normal (as in the comet and shubunkin) to egg-shaped (lionhead) or almost globular (veiltail). The caudal (tail) fin can resemble that of the wild ancestor or be elongated or duplicated. Twin-tailed varieties exhibit huge variations in the caudal fin. The top lobes can be separated or else partially or completed divided, while the whole tail can be relatively short or well-developed, spread out or trailing, with prominent or absent forking. Anal fins can be single, double, or absent, while the dorsal fin is typically normal, well-developed, or absent altogether.

The head and eyes

The shape of the head varies between varieties, but two very particular features will stand out: the hood (as in the lionhead) and the "narial bouquets," or "pompoms," which are enlarged nostril tissue. The extreme eye development of exotic goldfish causes some hobbyists to be apprehensive, although it probably does not bother the fish themselves. However, telescope-eyed goldfish, celestials (where the eyes point heavenwards), or bubble-eyed varieties (with delicate fluid-filled sacs billowing out beneath the eyes) do require special care; these fish may be bullied by other fish, injure themselves on sharp decor, or miss out on their full food rations.

Scales and pigmentation

Scales and pigmentation are very important in determining appearance. Normal, metallic goldfish possess reflective tissue (guanine) in the skin, but if this is absent the fish have a dull appearance and can appear scaleless. The individual scales of the pearlscaled goldfish have a hard deposit of calcium carbonate that resembles the dimples on a golf ball.

Left: The word "goldfish" does not do full justice to the many color variants. Chrome-yellow common goldfish such as this one waned in popularity, but are now being revived in the hobby – a case of "plain is beautiful".

Colors

The color of a goldfish is determined by the distribution and mixing of four pigments: black, red, yellow, and orange, and their depth in the skin layers. "Wild" fish lack orange and red; the standard goldfish retains only the red, while white fish lack all four pigments. Today's fancy goldfish can be single (self) colored, bi- or tricolored or so-called "calico", where red, black, white, orange, and blue pigments are all present. The best example of a calico fish is the shubunkin, which combines the five colors and many intermediate shades with dull scalation.

Maintaining goldfish in an aquarium

Since fancy goldfish all belong to the same species, they require essentially the same foods, water conditions, and accommodation. The information in this book pertaining to the "common" goldfish will thus apply to them all, and does not need repeating for each variety. There is some variation in size between the varieties, but water temperature and chemistry, diet and living space play just as great a part as genetics in deciding how big individual goldfish will grow. Deep-bodied varieties, such as the ryukin, require correspondingly deep tanks, and highly modified types, such as the celestial, are best kept only with others of their own kind, as their eyes are easily damaged.

While it is possible to keep one or two juvenile goldfish in the traditional bowl without filtration, this cruel practice should be discouraged. Just because goldfish are durable, this does not mean that they should be treated less well than any other cold water fish. In any case, learning how to maintain them properly is an excellent grounding in basic fishkeeping skills that will prepare you well if you want to try more demanding species.

Breeding goldfish

It is far easier to spawn goldfish in an outdoor pond than in an aquarium. Unless you study the subject in depth and start with good broodstock, there is little chance of ending up with much more than "mongrels," but it is still fun to bring on some home-growns, whatever their pedigree!

Do not expect goldfish to breed in a normal aquarium. You must keep the sexes separate and condition them with plenty of live foods, then bring them together to do their own thing in peace. However, the eggs and fry cannot be left to their own devices; they need to be saved from their cannibalistic parents and given special treatment. For this you will need one, and preferably two more tanks that each hold at least 20 gallons.

Below: A male common goldfish showing breeding tubercles. Cherish your broodstock, so that you can repeat pairings that result in particularly good batches of fry.

The breeding tank

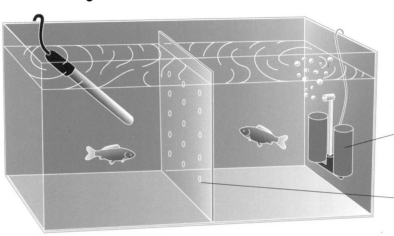

1 Feed the selected pair on nutritious live foods for some weeks, and gradually raise the water temperature to 75°F (24°C). The divider is perforated to allow full water circulation.

A simple sponge filter keeps the water sweet and grows microscopic food for subsequent fry.

Dividers can be made of any non-toxic plastic or mesh material.

2 For spawning, remove the divider and place a suitable medium (here a floating nylon fiber mop) in the tank. Disease-free natural plants can be used instead of, or in addition to, this.

Spawning takes place in the mop, with the male driving the female among the strands.

Remove the parents after spawning, otherwise the eggs will soon be eaten.

Choosing suitable fish

Confine your first spawning attempts to common goldfish or comets, as with these slim-bodied varieties it is easiest to see when the female is carrying developed eggs. She will become noticeably plump. Sexually mature males sometimes show spawning tubercles (pinhead-sized white pimples) on the gill covers and the leading edges of the pectoral fins, and their skin will become rough to the touch. (Do not confuse these pimples with white spot.)

The size of fish is less important than age in determining sexual maturity. Well-maintained goldfish that are two years old or more should be capable of spawning.

Spawning the fish

Summer is the best time to attempt spawning. Starting in early spring, separate the prospective parents in a bare 90–136 liter (20–30 gallon) filtered tank with a heater/thermostat and a divider down the middle. Site this in a quiet corner that receives the morning rays of the sun. Feed the goldfish on nutritious foods, including chopped earthworms, for several weeks, gradually raising the water temperature one degree at a time until it reaches 75°F (24°C). Then take out the divider and add a spawning medium, which can be real or artificial fine-leaved plants, boiled willow roots, or a mop made from strands of nylon fiber tied to a cork.

Be up early the next morning to witness the spawning. The male will drive the female into the mop or plants, where she will release adhesive eggs that he fertilizes. If no activity occurs within a day or two, replace the divider and try again after a week. If there is still no spawning activity, return the parent fish to their normal quarters, as repeated disruption will stress them.

Raising the fry

As soon as a spawning is finished, remove the adult goldfish immediately and maintain the water temperature at about 75°F (24°C). Fertile eggs are amber-colored and clear, while infertile ones quickly develop a fur coat of fungus and should be removed before they pollute the tank. The fry will hatch in three to four days and you can feed them two days later, once they have absorbed their yolk sacs. The easiest first food is a liquid preparation for egglaying fishes, followed in due course by newly hatched brine shrimp and, later, crumbled flakes. Their distended bellies will tell you if the young fish are getting enough, but do not overfeed them. A single spawning can result in up to 1000 eggs, so keep only the best of your fry to maturity, or you will quickly run out of rearing space.

Above: *When goldfish fry first start to feed, normal flake and live food is far too big for their tiny mouths and stomachs. Offer them a liquid diet (for egglayers), dripped into the tank. Do not overdo it, or you risk polluting the water.*

Right: These 48-hour-old fry resemble slivers of glass, but they will grow into shubunkins. At this stage, they cling to the aquarium glass, an easy meal for any larger fish.

COMMON GOLDFISH • *Carassius auratus*

FAMILY: CYPRINIDAE

The common goldfish is a typically "carp-shaped" fish, with paired pectoral and ventral fins and single dorsal, anal, and caudal fins. It exhibits no mutations of the eyes, finnage, head, or body, and apart from the color, is outwardly identical to the Asiatic wild form. It can grow to 30 cm (12 in) or more in outdoor ponds, but typically remains much smaller in the aquarium. Color is immensely variable, and commercial breeders are working on new permutations all the time. The typical example is a metallic red or orange, but common goldfish can also be chrome yellow, white, red/orange and white, red and black, or any combination of these colors. The panda, or magpie, is a black-and-white fish and gaining in popularity. Albino (red-eyed) and leucistic (black-eyed) colorless forms are uncommon, but sometimes available.

Sexing goldfish

Sexing is possible when the fish are in spawning condition; females round out and the males become rough to the touch, often with spawning tubercles on the head and leading edges of the pectoral fins. The belly of a female carrying eggs feels soft and flabby, compared to that of a male ready to shed milt (sperm).

Above: *These red-and-white common goldfish represent one color variant among many in what is, in terms of numbers kept, the world's most popular pet.*

Left: *Goldfish are truly international, with varieties developed in the Far East, Europe, and North America all having their devotees. It all started with this, the common goldfish.*

Origins

Central Europe, east to China and Korea, but introduced worldwide.

Ideal conditions

Water: Neutral to slightly alkaline, moderately hard to hard.

Temperature: 10–26°C (50–79°F).

Food: Goldfish are omnivores – they eat a wide range of plant matter and small aquatic invertebrates. Supplement commercial foods (flake, tablets, pellets, and foodsticks) with freeze-dried and frozen products, and offer safe live foods occasionally for variety. Obtain these only from ponds where there is no risk of introducing disease or parasites, or buy them from your pet store. Brine shrimp, whiteworm, and grindalworm can be cultured at home. Earthworms, fed chopped or whole, are entirely safe, and a great conditioning food prior to spawning. Offer vegetable matter (chopped lettuce, peas, and beans) sparingly. Restrict feedings to two small meals a day, and siphon out any uneaten food after 10–15 minutes.

Minimum number in the aquarium: 2.

Minimum tank size: 60 cm (24 in) for a young pair; correspondingly larger aquariums for larger groups or mature goldfish (adhere to recommended stocking levels – see page 13).

Tank region: Bottom, middle, and top.

Juvenile markings

Young common goldfish very often show attractive black markings on the back and fins, which disappear as they mature. Others never color up at all, remaining a uniform brown. These superficially resemble crucian carp.

Above: *Although white, this goldfish is not a true albino, as the eyes are black rather than red. Sometimes, with age, colored goldfish turn white, but still remain healthy specimens.*

Right: *This very deep-bodied young common goldfish will probably lose all the black markings as it matures. You can already see from the isolated black scales midway along the flanks that the dark pigment is migrating upwards.*

COMET

The comet is similar to the common goldfish, but slimmer-bodied, and with elongated fins and tail. The variety first appeared in the US in the late nineteenth century. It is a very active fish and needs plenty of swimming space. The red-and-white sarasa comet is particularly attractive. Many mass-produced farmed goldfish are an intermediate form between the comet and common varieties, and shubunkin blood has led to calico comets appearing in non-pedigree shipments. While these fish may never win prizes, their mixed ancestry makes them extremely hardy, so they are a good choice for the beginner.

Right: This fine example of a comet has a tail equal in length to the body. Rather than impeding swimming, the elongated finnage gives this variety a quick burst of speed.

Left: A sarasa comet is a white fish with red markings. The depth of the red has been greatly improved over the years, and now these fish rival the koi equivalent, the Kohaku, in beauty.

24

SHUBUNKINS (*London and Bristol*)

Shubunkins, another single-tailed variety, lack the guanine pigment in and beneath the scales, so their skin appears dull. They are generally calico (multi-colored) fish, although a modern development shows blue-black markings on a white ground, with the reds absent. The London shubunkin is similar in shape to the common goldfish, but with rounded ends to the tail. The Bristol shubunkin is longer-bodied, with more developed fins and a squared-off tail. Most shubunkins on sale generally are non-pedigree, and show finnage suggesting comet lineage. They can be aggressive to other fancy goldfish, chasing and fin-nipping their tankmates.

A London shubunkin combines functional body shape with beautiful calico colors.

Above: *A fine example of a Bristol shubunkin, a calico fish developed in the UK. With its pearly sheen, elongated but substantial single tail, and slim body, it is both beautiful and robust enough to hold its own in any mixed aquarium of fancy goldfish.*

Left: *Non-pedigree shubunkins are mass-farmed and may carry genes from other fancy goldfish varieties. This outcrossing produces hardy fish.*

MOOR

This metallic black, veiltailed goldfish has double caudal and anal fins and a flaglike dorsal. Two types of tail fin are recognized: the undivided broadtail, now rather uncommon, and the true veiltail. The body is high-backed and the eyes large and protuberant to varying degrees (described as telescope or "dragon" eyes). Ideally, moors are uniformly velvety-black, but poorer examples have a bronze tinge that becomes more pronounced with age. Like all short-bodied goldfish, they can be prone to swimbladder trouble unless kept warm and fed on live food with a high fiber content, such as daphnia. Despite their exotic appearance, moors are not particularly delicate and contrast well with the more colorful goldfish varieties.

Moors are among the first goldfish to show outward signs of skin parasites, as the excess mucus generated in response to them shows up as a gray film on the black fish.

There is just a hint of bronze color in the scales of the belly, a slight fault in strict competition terms.

Right: Black gold – finding a really good example of a moor is like striking oil. This particular fish has good finnage and body and the typical telescope eyes. This variety appreciates a slightly warm tank.

ORANDA

Orandas are short-bodied, high-backed fish, with long, paired fins, a high dorsal fin, and a characteristic hood growth covering the head. There are many color forms, including calico, blue, brown, black, chocolate, and the redcap, which has a white body and red head. Telescope-eyed orandas are a further variant. Orandas are sometimes confused with lionheads or the Japanese ranchu, but although all these fishes develop the head hood, lionheads lack a dorsal fin. Orandas are sedate swimmers, but be sure to provide a deep tank (45 cm/18 in or more in depth) for larger specimens.

Left: Redcap orandas are so called because of the color of the hood. The Japanese like these goldfish because the marking mimics that on the head of their national bird, the Tancho crane.

Above: A pair of red orandas with well-developed hoods moving down over the cheeks. Do not confuse these fish with lionheads or ranchu, which lack a dorsal fin (see page 31).

RYUKIN

Left: *This red-and-white ryukin is very typical of the variety, and the fins carried erect show it to be in good health. Feed it live foods to prevent swimbladder troubles from occurring.*

Below: *A charming tricolored ryukin. Improvements to a known variety very often focus on line-breeding for color, while retaining all the other desirable characteristics of finnage and body shape.*

The hardy ryukin (developed in 1680) is a very deep-bodied metallic fish with a somewhat pointed head, high dorsal fin, and pronounced shoulder hump. The tail fin is forked and divided, and there is a double anal fin. Color morphs are numerous, and include a calico variant.

A similar-looking fish is the tosakin (also known as the curly-tailed fantail). Here, the upper lobes of the twin caudal fin are joined and spread wide, while the lower lobes are curled. This is very much a show fish, best appreciated by viewing it from above. It is not as good a swimmer as the ryukin, and is considered to be rather delicate.

FANTAIL

A "fantail" describes a physical attribute shared by several varieties of fancy goldfish, but it is also a variety in its own right. Imagine a ryukin's egg-shaped body without the shoulder hump and with rather less exaggerated paired finnage, and you have a fantail, which was developed to suit the Western taste in fancy goldfish.

Fantails can be nacreous (pearly) or metallic (calico and bronze are popular colors). Telescope-eyes are permitted. Another very similar variety is the jikin. When viewed directly from behind, its tail resembles a butterfly with spread wings.

Below: A classic orange fantail. The paired, elongated caudal fins are held quite stiffly away from the body and do not droop at all.

Above: This is a nice example of a red-and-white fantail. The first (hard) spine of the dorsal fin is clearly shown — its crookedness could be genetic or the result of careless handling in transit.

VEILTAIL

This is another fancy goldfish variety "born in the USA". As the name suggests, the divided caudal fin is greatly elongated and trails down like a curtain. The body is almost spherical and the dorsal fin is prominent and carried high. Eyes can be normal or telescopic, and a number of colors, single or in combination, are recognized. The term "veiltail" is used more generally to describe any non-specific fancy goldfish with a trailing caudal fin, and many mass-produced specimens show tail development that falls between the fantail and veiltail.

Right: This all-orange veiltail shows clearly why deep tanks are necessary for the variety. Only then will the fish carry itself properly. Note the broad, almost squared-off tail and greatly elongated pectoral and pelvic fins.

Left: Elongated finnage develops quite early in veiltails, so that younger specimens such as this one can appear out of proportion. Keep this variety with other long-finned goldfish, rather than active varieties such as shubunkins.

LIONHEAD and RANCHU

These varieties are similar to look at, and the names are frequently interchanged. However, strictly speaking, a lionhead is a fish developed by the Chinese, while the ranchu is the same fish taken in a slightly different direction by the Japanese. Both give an impression of strength, and the alternative common name of "buffalo-head" is very apt, since a well-developed hood does suggest the head of a plains bison! The hood can cover the top of the head only, or extend over the cheeks, or completely encase the head, cheeks, and gill covers. Generally speaking, the older the fish, the more pronounced the hood will be.

Lionheads and ranchus are reputed to be delicate, but hobbyists specializing in these fish report that they can spend much of the year in outdoor ponds, even in temperate climates.

Both varieties have a short, deep body, with a smoothly arched back and no dorsal fin. Poor examples sometimes show a vestigial dorsal, or a bump or depression where the fin should be. Other fins are short, and the anal fins are paired. The double caudal fin (a fantail) is quite short; in the lionhead it does not droop, but is held stiffly away from the body. The tail of the ranchu is similar, but because the thick caudal peduncle takes a sharper downward curve from the body, the tail adopts a lower profile.

Numerous color varieties (nacreous and metallic) have been developed, including calico (known as edonishiki) and black. Lionheads and ranchu have a rather stiff swimming motion, but only if the hood extends down over the eyes do they appear to have any difficulty holding their own with other goldfish varieties in the aquarium.

Below: This is a high-quality Japanese ranchu with good hood development, no suggestion of a dorsal fin, and a strong caudal peduncle (tail wrist). Appreciation societies for this variety exist worldwide.

Right: The whitish hood on this young lionhead already covers the head and cheeks and extends down either side of the mouth. The smooth back contour is a plus.

PEARLSCALE

This fantailed variety has an almost spherical body, with double caudal and anal fins. The scales that give the fish its name have individual raised deposits of calcium carbonate, causing the dimpled effect of a golfball (or halved pearls). This phenomenon also mutes the underlying colors, which appear pale or pastel. Strangely, if any scales are lost, the replacements grow back as normal scalation.

Pearlscales are very susceptible to swimbladder problems, because the rounded body compresses and distorts the organ of balance. Do not keep them below 13°C (55°F), as chilling only makes the problem worse.

Right: This pearlscale has a striking combination of a yellow body and black fins. New color patterns are constantly under development in the goldfish hobby.

Below: This red-and-white pearlscale clearly shows the "dimpling" caused by the calcium deposits in the center of each scale. Finnage is similar to that of the fantail goldfish.

POMPOM

A pompom is both a variety in its own right and a feature found in other fancy goldfish variants. The pompom proper resembles a lionhead, but instead of the characteristic hood there are fleshy narial growths between the nostrils. In good specimens, these look rather like the pompoms carried by cheerleaders.

The pompom nasal feature is also found on some veiltails and orandas. The growths can be of a contrasting color to the body; for example, a brown veiltail with red pompoms looks quite dramatic.

Well-developed narial growths waving about as the pompom swims around the aquarium can be irresistible to some other goldfish, so watch for any signs of damage.

Right: *Chocolate pompom veiltails with orange narial bouquets offer a pleasing color contrast. This variety (also known as Chairo Hanafusa) has the typical oranda's high dorsal fin, whereas in the pompom proper this fin is absent.*

With its eyes turned heavenward, the celestial is one of the more extreme fancy goldfish varieties. It is twin-tailed, with no dorsal fin, and the caudal fins can be either short or quite elongated. Celestials have "telescope" eyes that migrate upward as the fish mature. This obviously means that their vision is restricted. Because they would have difficulty competing for food with normally sighted goldfish, they are generally kept only with their own kind.

Right: The first fancy goldfish were kept in opaque ceramic bowls, and direct eye contact with their owners was possible only with this variety.

Right: Celestials begin life looking much like other goldfish, but the eyes soon start to migrate around the head until they are facing directly upward. The recessive gene causing this feature would never have survived long in nature.

Along with the tail-less meteor, the bubble-eye is taking selective breeding to the outer limits, and many fans of fancy goldfish draw the line at keeping a variety so far removed from the original genetic blueprint. The body and finnage is like that of the lionhead, but beneath each eye is a fluid-filled sac, or bladder, that wobbles as the fish swims. The larger these sacs are, the more the eyes are displaced upward. Good specimens should have symmetrical sacs, but very often they are of unequal size, which makes swimming even more difficult for these fish.

The sacs are very prone to damage, so make sure the aquarium is free of any sharp gravel or decor, and do not mix the bubble-eyes with more agile goldfish. The variety is produced in a number of single colors or color combinations, including calico and black.

Right: In this trio of bubble-eyes, the sacs are so well-developed that they restrict swimming. Note the rounded gravel that prevents damage to these delicate fish.

Fish for cool tanks

The species featured on pages 37–59 open up endless possibilities for the aquarium keeper. All can be housed in an unheated tank, as they originate from the temperate regions of Europe and North America. Those on sale in pet stores are both colorful and undemanding – the majority are members of the carp family (Cyprinidae), which are easy to feed and very peaceful, even at spawning time. But fish are not kept for their looks alone. The breeding behavior of the stickleback, bullhead, and the various sunfish is fascinating to observe, and researching the correct conditions for spawning to occur is challenging and rewarding.

Into this section fall several species you can collect from the wild, and details of how to do this are given on page 10. It is amazing how apparently insignificant native fish can develop personalities all their own when you care for them on a daily basis. Some fish will be difficult to obtain, due either to import restrictions or seasonal availability. Find a pet store specializing in out-of-the-ordinary fish and the staff will help you find what you want. Or join a club or society – these can be excellent sources of unusual home-bred fish. Never release fish from another country into the wild: they can easily upset the ecological balance.

Right: Cold water fish span all extremes of habitat – from stagnant ponds to rushing mountain streams like this, where the water is highly oxygenated.

BLEAK ● *Alburnus alburnus*

FAMILY: CYPRINIDAE

The nacreous scales of the bleak were once the raw material of a thriving artificial pearl industry, as the sides of these locally abundant fish shine bright silver and reflect the light. Bleak are active, surface-feeding schoolers, heavily preyed on by pike, perch, and zander. They are useful in a large, well-aerated community cold water aquarium, as they occupy the upper layers of the water. Keep the tank well-covered, as they are great jumpers.

Although healthy specimens will thrive, bleak are quite delicate and prone to transit damage, so choose your stock carefully.

Origins

United Kingdom, mainland Europe, Asia.

The upturned mouth of the bleak rightly suggests that it spends most of its time at or near the surface. Note the very long anal fin.

Ideal conditions

Water: Neutral, slightly hard.
Temperature: 8–20°C (46–68°F).
Food: Aquatic and surface-blown insects. Will take flake, daphnia, and freeze-dried mosquito larvae.
Minimum number in the aquarium: 6.
Minimum tank size: 90 cm (36 in).
Tank region: Middle and top.

FAMILY: CYPRINIDAE

This very close relative of the goldfish is often mistaken for the "brown" goldfish that are produced in all spawnings, but the profile of the crucian's dorsal fin is convex, rather than concave. The two species readily hybridize, and pure-bred crucians are becoming uncommon as a result.

Origins

Eastern England to central Russia, but widely introduced elsewhere.

Crucian carp make ideal aquarium inhabitants, their brassy sides more apparent than in a pond. Spawning behavior, feeding requirements, and general husbandry are exactly the same as for the goldfish, although crucians are arguably even hardier, able to withstand great temperature variations and water with a low dissolved oxygen content. These pleasing little fish will grow only to the confines of their tank. In the wild, they quickly overpopulate a pond and stunted, though perfectly healthy, populations result.

▶ Ideal conditions

Water: Neutral, moderately hard.
Temperature: 10–25°C (50–77°F).
Food: Flake, frozen, or freeze-dried foods, floating foodsticks, plus worms and daphnia are all eagerly taken.
Minimum number in the aquarium: 2.
Minimum tank size: 60 cm (24 in).
Tank region: Bottom, middle.

Crucian carp and goldfish have no mouth barbels, unlike the two pairs on koi. But hybrids with Cyprinus carpio do occur, in which barbels may or may not be present.

This fish clearly shows the convex dorsal fin that marks it as a true crucian, not just an uncolored goldfish. The body of the crucian carp tends to be deeper, too.

GUDGEON ● *Gobio gobio*

FAMILY: CYPRINIDAE

Gudgeon resemble a miniature version of the barbel *(Barbus barbus* – see page 70), but have only one, as opposed to two, pairs of whiskers (also known as barbels). They inhabit rivers, streams, and stillwaters, but prefer a swift current over a gravel bottom, where they form dense schools. Their coloration is subtle, rather than spectacular; when light falls on their sides, iridescent blues and purples contrast pleasingly with the distinct scale reticulation. Males develop head tubercles in the breeding season.

These peaceful little fish will share an aquarium with other European species. Despite their modest size, they are strong and well adapted to fast-flowing habitats. Set up the aquarium with good water circulation over a substrate of fine, rounded gravel or river sand, and larger rocks to provide cover.

Gudgeon parties

In the nineteenth century, boating parties used to fish for gudgeon on the Thames River. An area of river bed would first be raked over and thousands of worms introduced to get the fish in the mood for feeding. The catch (ladies fished as well as men) was then fried on the river bank!

Ideal conditions

Water: Neutral, moderately hard.
Temperature: 10–18°C (50–64°F).
Food: Insect larvae, worms, small aquatic mollusks. Feed freeze-dried or frozen equivalents, along with live daphnia and bloodworm. Can be weaned on to flake food.
Minimum number in the aquarium: 4.
Minimum tank size: 75 cm (30 in).
Tank region: Bottom.

Gudgeon have a steeper head profile than the barbel, and much larger eyes.

Origins

Widespread across mainland Europe and the UK, except Cornwall and the Lake District, where they are uncommon.

BLUEHEAD CHUB • *Nocomis leptocephalus*

FAMILY: CYPRINIDAE

In Europe, only one fish – *Leuciscus cephalus* – is known as the chub, but in the United States this common name is applied to several cyprinid species. The bluehead is rarely imported, as its somewhat "heavy-headed" appearance is not to everyone's taste. However, it exhibits interesting breeding behavior. Young specimens display a dark line along the sides and a caudal spot, both of which fade on maturity.

To get the best from blueheads, they need a spacious, planted aquarium, with a largely sandy substrate interspersed with areas of gravel, which is used in nest-building. At breeding time, males develop prominent tubercles, and the area between the eyes becomes raised and thickened. This species is very intolerant of poor water quality.

Ideal conditions

Water: Neutral, slightly hard.
Temperature: 10–20°C (50–68°F).
Food: Small live or frozen aquatic invertebrates and some plant matter. Can be weaned on to flake foods.
Minimum number in the aquarium: 4.
Minimum tank size: 90 cm (36 in).
Tank region: Middle to bottom.

Origins

Atlantic and Gulf Coast streams in the US.

Right: The typical habitat of the bluehead – a clean, medium-paced stream with a gravel bottom.

Breeding

In early summer, males construct a large, domed nest of stones and gravel up to 1 m (39 in) across. After a female has been lured inside and her several hundred eggs fertilized, the male guards these and the subsequent fry. If you wish to try this at home, provide a tank measuring at least 90x60x60 cm (36x24x24 in). Fry will require newly hatched brine shrimp as a first food.

Sensory pits on the head of this male bluehead help it locate food items in the substrate.

GOLDEN SHINER • *Notomigonus crysoleucas*

FAMILY: CYPRINIDAE

Golden shiners are not highly regarded in their country of origin, where they are more likely to be used as bait fish than aquarium stock. Nevertheless, they are graceful, schooling fish, predominantly metallic silver with a hint of gold where the light strikes their sides. Males develop orange-tinted ventral and anal fins during the spring spawning season. Eggs are scattered among plants in shallow water.

It is best to keep a school of at least six young specimens in a large tank with a sand or gravel substrate, rocks, bogwood, and tough-leaved plants. Golden shiners prefer gentle filtration.

The torpedo-shaped body of the golden shiner indicates a fast swimmer – a necessary requirement when a fish is a target for predators.

Origins

Medium-paced streams and rivers in eastern North America, from southern Canada to the Gulf Coast.

Ideal conditions

Water: Neutral, moderately hard.
Temperature: 10–20°C (50—68°F).
Food: Small live or frozen items, including freeze-dried mosquito larvae, which will be taken from the surface. Flake, small floating pellets and some plant matter (algae wafers).
Minimum number in the aquarium: 4, preferably a school of 6.
Minimum tank size: 90 cm (36 in).
Tank region: Middle, top.

SHINER • *Notropis lutrensis*

FAMILY: CYPRINIDAE

This native North American species is widely imported into Europe for the aquarium trade and is an ideal choice for anyone wishing to try something a bit different from goldfish. Its requirements are very similar.

The sexes are easy to tell apart. Males are stockier than females and much more colorful, with orange fins and heads and a bluish iridescence on the sides that gives them their common name. In an aquarium that catches the rays of the morning sun, they can rival tropical characins for brilliance. These peaceful fish tolerate a wide range of temperatures and can be kept in a community setup, but look their best when seen as a large school in a species tank.

Furnish the aquarium with plants and inert rockwork over a stony or gravelled substrate. These fish appreciate a moderately fast current, which you can provide from an internal power filter or powerheads.

Ideal conditions

Water: Neutral to slightly alkaline, slightly to moderately hard.
Temperature: 15–24°C (59–75°F).
Food: Live, flake, or frozen food, with some plant matter.
Minimum number in the aquarium: 6.
Minimum tank size: 90 cm (36 in).
Tank region: Bottom, middle, and top.

Left: A pair of well-conditioned shiners, with the male above showing characteristic breeding tubercles on the head. These are typical egg-scatterers: reports of aquarium breeding are rare.

Origins

Midwestern United States.

The iridescent sides justify the common name of "shiner." This is a popular aquarium choice on both sides of the Atlantic.

SOUTHERN REDBELLY DACE ● *Phoxinus erythrogaster*

FAMILY: CYPRINIDAE

Phoxinus erythrogaster is very similar to the European minnow (*P. phoxinus* - see page 44) in appearance and aquarium requirements, but is even more colorful. It is frequently imported into Europe. Both sexes have iridescent sides and the males may have yellow or bright red bellies at spawning time, with head tubercles that can be easily mistaken for white spot parasites. The males show off their best colors in a school containing both sexes. They prefer temperatures at the lower end of the tolerance scale and a planted aquarium with a sand or gravel substrate, impeccable water quality, and a fast current. Suitable tankmates are loaches, gudgeon, and bullheads. The fish scatter their eggs over gravel in the shallows during spring and early summer. There is no brood care.

Origins

Widespread in streams and well-paced rivers across central US.

The pastel colors of the northern redbelly dace are reflected in its specific name "eos" (Phoxinus eos), which means "dawn."

Do not overwhelm small fish like these with large tankmates, however peaceful. Your aquarium will look unbalanced.

▶ *Ideal conditions*

Water: Slightly acidic to neutral, slightly soft.
Temperature: 10–20°C (50–68°F).
Food: Mainly small live foods, such as daphnia, bloodworm, and cyclops, but can be persuaded to take flake.
Minimum number in the aquarium: 6.
Minimum tank size: 75 cm (30 in).
Tank region: Bottom, middle, and top.

EUROPEAN MINNOW • *Phoxinus phoxinus*

FAMILY: CYPRINIDAE

Minnows make up a large percentage of the diet of kingfishers, and are also preyed upon by chub, pike, perch, asp (a predatory member of the carp family), and zander (pikeperch found in central Europe). They are found wherever there is well-oxygenated water with a clean sand or gravel substrate, but are highly intolerant of pollution. These fish are unhappy if kept in twos and threes, as in the wild they form small schools, often in the company of gudgeon, to search for food. This schooling behavior provides protection from predators.

In spring, mature males develop head tubercles and bright red bellies, and the golden side stripe becomes even more pronounced. Minnows are quite undemanding to keep, providing you maintain good water quality. A strong current over a gravel bottom, with plant and rock cover, suits them best. They can be mixed with other, similarly sized fishes.

Origins

Widespread in streams and rivers across Northern Europe.

Choose healthy fish that carry their dorsal fin erect, as here. The branched fin rays can be clearly seen.

Ideal conditions

Water: Slightly acidic to slightly alkaline, slightly soft to slightly hard.
Temperature: 8–20°C (46–68°F).
Food: Small live or frozen aquatic invertebrates, including daphnia and mosquito larvae. Algae wafers. Tablet food and flake.
Minimum number in the aquarium: 6.
Minimum tank size: 60 cm (24 in).
Tank region: Bottom, middle, and top.

For such small fish, European minnows are very long-lived – up to 10 years – in captivity.

ROSY RED MINNOW ● *Pimephales promelas*

FAMILY: CYPRINIDAE

This fish is a close relative of the bluntnose minnow *(Pimephales notatus)*, but while the bluntnose is a green-backed, silvery fish, the rosy red minnow is a lovely salmon pink. In recent years, *P. promelas* has been a popular export to Europe, where its small size and wide temperature tolerance has made it an ideal fish for outdoor ponds, as well as aquariums. It breeds readily in captivity and, unusually for cyprinids, males of both species exhibit brood care.

Rosy red minnows are best kept in large schools in well-established tanks. Provide a substrate of fine gravel or sand, some plant cover, and breeding caves made from upturned flowerpots with an entrance hole made in the side.

Ideal conditions

Water: Slightly acidic to slightly alkaline, slightly soft to slightly hard.
Temperature: 10–20°C (50–68°F).
Food: All small live, freeze-dried, and frozen foods. Live bloodworm is a good conditioner prior to spawning. Provide some green food, either fresh (lettuce, cucumber) or prepared (algae wafers).
Minimum number in the aquarium: 6.
Minimum tank size: 75 cm (30 in).
Tank region: Middle, top.

The scales of the bluntnose minnow are small and easily damaged on sharp tank decor.

Origins
Rivers and streams in central US.

Pimephales promelas *originates from the US and is now commercially bred there and in the Far East.*

Breeding

The male first clears an area beneath a flat rock or upturned flowerpot, then displays with flared fins to his chosen female, who lays 100 or more eggs on the roof of the "cave." These, and the subsequent fry, are guarded by the male, who will defend his territory against intruders. Luckily, he is not equipped to do them much damage. The youngsters can be raised on infusoria as a first food, followed by newly hatched brine shrimp.

RUDD • *Scardinius erythrophthalmus*

Size: Males and females 40 cm (16 in), but usually smaller

FAMILY: CYPRINIDAE

Unlike the roach, the very similar rudd is bred in a golden form, mainly for pond collections. However, a school of youngsters makes an impressive display in a large aquarium. They are surface-feeding, active fish, and even the wild form has bronze or yellow sides. The cultivated variety is colored deep orange, with varying amounts of greenish brown, mainly on the back.

Rudd need a deep, sheltered aquarium with a fine gravel substrate and plenty of cover, but they may eat natural plants, so plastic ones are a safer option. In the wild, they live in slow-moving rivers and lakes, so in the aquarium provide good filtration without creating strong currents.

In the wild, rudd spawn in typical cyprinid egg-scattering fashion from April to June. The adhesive eggs stick to aquatic plants. Spawning is possible in a large species aquarium.

This is the golden rudd, a more colorful variety than the wild form. Golden tench, orfe, and carp are also available, but more suitable for keeping in a pond.

The dorsal fin of the rudd is set farther back than in the roach, and the lower jaw is more prominent.

Ideal conditions

Water: Neutral, moderately hard.
Temperature: 10–20°C (50–68°F).
Food: Will take frozen and freeze-dried foods, with a preference for those that float or sink slowly, such as dried mosquito larvae. Larger specimens need vegetable matter in their diet (shredded lettuce and algae wafers).
Minimum number in the aquarium: 4.
Minimum tank size: 90 cm (36 in).
Tank region: Middle, top.

Origins

The UK and mainland Europe, south to Greece.

46

PYGMY SUNFISH • *Elassoma evergladei*

FAMILY: CENTRARCHIDAE (SUNFISH)

Sunfish can be quite aggressive and demanding of space, but these charming fish are the exception. They have a wide geographical distribution, and southern populations may need to be kept at the higher end of the suggested temperature band. Despite their diminutive size (and because of it), they are suited only to tanks containing others of their own kind. At spawning time, males become quite territorial and will defend their nests regardless of the size of the intruder.

Sexes are very similar except in the breeding season, when the fins of the males turn a deep black. The pygmy sunfish inhabits waters with heavy plant growth and bottom detritus (including the Florida Everglades), and the tank should be set up accordingly, with plenty of cover in the form of rocks and roots. Gentle but efficient filtration is vital.

Origins

Still or slow-moving waters in North America, from North Carolina to Florida.

Breeding

In order to breed these fish the following spring, keep them cool over winter and condition them on live foods. Unless you can provide plenty of space, select just one pair for the breeding tank. The male guards the 50 or so eggs in a shallow pit dug in the sand or gravel substrate. Fry are tiny and need microworm or newly hatched brine shrimp as first foods.

Ideal conditions

Water: Neutral to slightly alkaline, slightly soft.
Temperature: 10–30°C (50–86°F).
Food: Small items of live food (except tubifex), including whiteworm, chopped earthworms, daphnia, and crayfish. Some plant matter in the form of vegetable flake or algae wafers. May show reluctance to feed when first acquired.
Minimum number in the aquarium: 4.
Minimum tank size: 75 cm (30 in).
Tank region: Bottom, middle, and top.

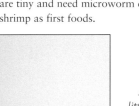

Although a little scrappy at breeding time, the pygmy sunfish is the ideal beginner's choice from this family of perch-like fish.

BLUE-SPOTTED SUNFISH ● *Enneacanthus gloriosus*

FAMILY: CENTRARCHIDAE (SUNFISH)

Like many fish species that show brood care, this sunfish is deceptively peaceful until spawning time, when the males will fight anything that approaches the nest. Young specimens are banded, which offers camouflage against predators, but these markings disappear as the fish mature. Females lack the dark opercular (gill) spots of the males.

Be careful to adjust the pH of your aquarium to that of the dealer's water, otherwise these fish can succumb to fungal infections. For the same reason, conduct small but regular partial water changes, rather than large and infrequent ones.

The tank should be heavily filtered to maintain good water quality. Direct the return flow from power filters against the back glass, to reduce turbulence. Provide plenty of natural plant cover with caves, interspersed with open areas of fine river gravel.

Breeding

Provide a large tank (120 cm/48 in or more) for the breeding of no more than two pairs of blue-spotted sunfish. They are typical pit spawners that benefit from a cooling period over winter to bring them into condition (see page 47). Allow the water temperature to rise naturally in spring by placing the tank where it receives some morning sunlight.

Origins
New York State, and down the eastern seaboard of the US to Florida.

The blue-spotted sunfish shows a characteristic "ear-shaped" spot on the top leading edge of the operculum.

Ideal conditions

Water: Neutral to slightly alkaline, slightly soft to slightly hard.
Temperature: 10–20°C (50–68°F), but with no sudden fluctuations.
Food: The fish prefer live food items, including bloodworm, daphnia, and crayfish, but can be persuaded to take flake and carnivore pellets.
Minimum number in the aquarium: 4.
Minimum tank size: 90 cm (36 in), but 120 cm (48 in) for breeding.
Tank region: Bottom, middle, and top.

Common names for fish can be confusing – the marine "sunfish", Mola mola, is huge and completely unrelated to the Centrarchidae. Always use the scientific name where possible, as then everyone is speaking the same language!

DIAMOND SUNFISH ● *Enneacanthus obesus*

FAMILY: CENTRARCHIDAE (SUNFISH)

The scientific name of this fish confirms that it has a rather rotund body shape, and indeed it is not the most active of sunfish species. It sometimes buries itself so that only the eyes are above the substrate, possibly to ambush food.

The behavior and water requirements of *E. obesus* are much the same as for the blue-spotted sunfish and it is equally intolerant of sudden changes in water chemistry or poor water quality. The tank should be mature and well furnished with plants, rocks, and bogwood over a fine substrate, into which they dig spawning pits.

Origins

Eastern seaboard of the US, from New England down to Florida.

Ideal conditions

Water: Neutral to slightly alkaline, slightly soft to slightly hard.
Temperature: 10–20°C (50–68°F).
Food: Live food that wriggles and hops, including bloodworm, daphnia, and crayfish. Will take flake and carnivore pellets. Vary the diet so that the fish do not become dependent on a particular item.
Minimum number in the aquarium: 4.
Minimum tank size: 90 cm (36 in), but 120 cm (48 in) for breeding.
Tank region: Bottom, middle, and top.

The quiet one

The black-banded sunfish, Enneacanthus chaetodon (shown here), has a water temperature preference of 4–20°C (39–68°F), in keeping with its distribution throughout New York State, Maryland, and New Jersey, where winters can be harsh. It grows to only 10 cm (4 in) in length and is quite shy, best kept only with its own kind in a quiet, planted aquarium. It is likely to accept only small live foods, such as daphnia, and requires lots of gentle, regular maintenance to avoid sudden fluctuations in temperature or water chemistry. This species is a pit-spawner, the male guarding the eggs and fry.

Many predatory fish carry a vertical stripe through the eye, to disguise an otherwise giveaway feature from their potential prey.

GREEN SUNFISH • *Lepomis cyanellus*

Size: Males and females 20 cm (8 in)

FAMILY: CENTRARCHIDAE (SUNFISH)

Despite an apparently wide temperature tolerance and habitat range, this species appreciates warmer summer quarters than most other sunfish. However, it can be overwintered at 10°C (50°F). The lightly banded sides and leading edges of the dorsal, anal, and caudal fins shine like jewels as they catch the light.

These fish display the typical sunfish dual personality – meek outside the breeding season, but pugnacious and fearless when guarding eggs or fry. The bigger the tank you can provide, the better the chances that similar-sized tankmates will have of staying outside territorial boundaries.

The "alert" pose, typical of a predatory fish waiting for prey to come past. The finnage and body shape are all-purpose, as benefits a fish that is both hunter and hunted.

This prodigious mouth will deal with the largest earthworm.

Origins
Slow-moving or still waters from Canada right down to Mexico, east of the Rocky Mountains.

Sunfish defend a territory when they are breeding.

Ideal conditions

Water: Neutral to slightly alkaline, slightly soft to slightly hard.
Temperature: 15–22°C (59–72°F).
Food: Live, flake, and frozen foods are all accepted. Chopped earthworms will quickly bring the fish into breeding condition.
Minimum number in the aquarium: 4.
Minimum tank size: 90 cm (36 in), but larger for breeding.
Tank region: Bottom, middle, and top.

50

BLUEGILL • *Lepomis macrochirus*

FAMILY: CENTRARCHIDAE (SUNFISH)

Better known as a lesser sportfish than an aquarium occupant, this is nevertheless a very attractive sunfish, with a steely blue-gray body and fins. Against this background, the ear-shaped opercular spot stands out clearly.

For its size, it is quite peaceful (except, inevitably, at spawning time). The main problem with keeping this species is persuading it to feed. It is a carnivore that will almost never accept flake or frozen foods, and live foods can be hard to obtain all year round.

Origins

United States, from Ohio south to Arkansas and Kentucky.

If you keep sunfish, it's a good idea to cultivate a worm farm. In this way, you will always have a ready supply of protein-packed live food.

The adaptable pumpkinseed

The pumpkinseed sunbass (Lepomis gibbosus) is well-traveled from its natural haunts across the US, with isolated breeding populations in southern England. It is less aggressive than other family members, but needs quite a large tank, as it grows to 20 cm (8 in). Breeding may occur – the male digs a large pit in the substrate and guards the eggs and fry. Remove the female after spawning. The common name reflects the elliptical body shape. It will take frozen foods and flake, though the natural diet is aquatic insects and small fish.

▶ Ideal conditions

Water: Neutral to slightly alkaline, slightly to moderately hard.
Temperature: 4–21°C (39–70°F).
Food: Exclusively live food, such as crayfish, worms, daphnia, and glassworm. Will prey on fry of its own and other species.
Minimum number in the aquarium: 2.
Minimum tank size: 90 cm (36 in).
Tank region: Bottom, middle, and top.

BLACK CRAPPIE ● *Pomoxis nigromaculatus*

FAMILY: CENTRARCHIDAE (SUNFISH)

This pleasingly shaped but rather robust fish has gained favor among fishermen. The black crappie actually sports a dappled pattern against a metallic yellowish ground color, which is seen at its best when light strikes its side laterally. An aquarium with a dark background and substrate show it off well.

This species is only for the enthusiast. As a youngster it is quite peaceful, but as it grows, it will prey on any other fish that will fit into its rather wide mouth. It is an active swimmer, particularly toward dusk, when it does most of its feeding.

The usual sunfish criteria of a spacious, well-filtered, and planted tank apply. A 120 cm (48 in) aquarium will house one adult pair.

Scientific names usually give a clue to the appearance or behavior of a fish. "Nigromaculatus" translates from the Latin as "black-spotted."

> ## Ideal conditions

Water: Slightly acidic to slightly alkaline, slightly hard.
Temperature: 10–20°C (50–68°F).
Food: Shrimp, crayfish, worms, fish, and some plant matter.
Minimum number in the aquarium: 2.
Minimum tank size: 120 cm (48 in).
Tank region: Bottom, middle, and top.

The dappled pattern carried into the fins breaks up the outline of the fish when it is resting amid shadowy plant thickets.

Origins

Rivers and stillwaters across eastern and central United States.

BULLHEAD • *Cottus gobio*

FAMILY: COTTIDAE

"Fierce-looking" describes this homely but harmless little fish, whose other common name of "miller's thumb" acknowledges its very broad head. It spends most of its time under stones in fast-flowing stretches of water, ambushing food items swept down by the current. It spreads its broad pectoral fins to give it stability and during courtship displays, but it is not a strong swimmer. If you can provide a cool, well-aerated tank with a strong flow across the substrate, bullheads are easy to keep with similarly sized British native fish. They can be quite difficult to spot on a sand and coarse gravel substrate, a protective measure against predators. Water quality must be beyond reproach, as bullheads die if conditions are anything but perfect. Change at least 20% of the tank water every week.

An American cousin

The North American Cottus bairdi, shown here, is a close relative of the European bullhead, and, not surprisingly, the two species have very similar living requirements and breeding habits. This brightly marked specimen clearly shows the huge spreading pectoral fins, used to fan the eggs. In the United States the word "bullhead" is more commonly applied to native catfishes.

Origins

Clean streams and rivers across the UK and mainland Europe.

Ideal conditions

Water: Neutral to slightly alkaline, slightly soft to slightly hard.
Temperature: 10–20°C (50–68°F).
Food: Small invertebrates, such as damsel nymphs and stonefly larvae. In captivity, they take flake, frozen, and live foods, especially small worms.
Minimum number in the aquarium: 4.
Minimum tank size: 45 cm (18 in).
Tank region: Bottom.

Breeding

If flat stones or caves are available, bullheads will spawn in spring and early summer. A clutch of 50–100 large orange eggs are laid in shallow water and guarded by the male.

FAMILY: GASTEROSTEIDAE

The dorsal spines of the familiar "tiddler" are an ideal defense against being swallowed, and males of this schooling species are bolder than fish many times their size. Three-spined sticklebacks are well worth keeping in a small species aquarium, both for their appearance (breeding males have red bellies, bluish green backs, and blue eyes) and spawning behavior.

Sticklebacks require a well-furnished tank with plenty of plant and rock cover and good, but gentle, filtration. A rock with a growth of willow moss *(Fontinalis antipyretica)* will be picked at to provide nesting material, or you could use Java moss.

If you catch your own fish, avoid specimens with very plump bellies, as this indicates parasitic worm infestation, which is very common in sticklebacks. Stock in the ratio of one male to three or four females and do not overcrowd the tank, otherwise the males will constantly squabble.

Origins

Fresh and brackish water in Europe, northern Asia and the US.

Prominent spines are purely for protection against predators – males do not use them in territorial squabbles.

Breeding

In spring, the male stakes out a territory, builds a domed nest of plant material, and lures in several females in succession to spawn, driving them through the entrance and fertilizing the eggs. He jealously guards and defends the resulting 50 or so eggs and the subsequent "pinhead" fry.

Ideal conditions

Water: Neutral, slightly to moderately hard.
Temperature: 4–18°C (39–64°F).
Food: Live aquatic invertebrates and small worms, chopped if necessary. May also take carnivore flake and freeze-dried mosquito larvae.
Minimum number in the aquarium: 4 (3 males, 1 female).
Minimum tank size: 45 cm (18 in).
Tank region: Bottom, middle, and top.

Ten-spined stickleback

This fish is smaller and able to tolerate brackish water. It is not as easy to keep as its close relative, because it is much choosier about diet and unlikely to accept flake food.

RAINBOW DARTER • *Etheostoma caeruleum*

Family: Percidae (Perches)

Darters are a large genus of fish endemic to the United States, but rarely imported into Europe. Many are highly localized or endangered by disappearing habitat, but the more common species make ideal tank inhabitants, providing you create and maintain first-rate water quality.

Darters are bottom-dwellers, and their common name derives from the way they move jerkily over the substrate, using their caudal and pectoral fins. Males are more colorful than females. They spawn in spring and early summer in depressions in the gravel, where they may deposit up to 1000 eggs.

Origins

Clean rivers and streams in Eastern US, especially the Mississippi Basin.

Propped up on its wide pectoral fins, this alert darter is not built for sustained swimming but for swift, evasive movements.

Ideal conditions

Water: Neutral, slightly soft to slightly hard.
Temperature: 6–15°C (42–59°F).
Food: Small aquatic invertebrates. May be persuaded to take freeze-dried mosquito larvae.
Minimum number in the aquarium: 4.
Minimum tank size: 75 cm (30 in).
Tank region: Bottom.

RUFFE, POPE, OR BLACKTAIL • *Gynocephalus cernua*

Size: *Males and females 25 cm (10 in), but usually smaller*

FAMILY: PERCIDAE (PERCHES)

The colors of this fish are subtle, rather than spectacular, although the mauve iris of the eye is quite attractive. Unlike its close cousin the perch, the ruffe is not a fish predator, but a bottom-grubber of aquatic insects. However, it will eat the spawn of other fish. In spring, it lays adhesive eggs on plants in the shallows. The first dorsal fin is spiny, the second soft-rayed. Leading rays of the lower fins also carry spines, and the gill covers have sharp edges, so handle this fish with care!

Origins

Slow-moving rivers in Central and Eastern England, Europe, Asia.

Typical of perches is the twin dorsal fin, the first spiny and the second soft-rayed.

Ideal conditions

Water: Neutral, slightly soft to slightly hard.
Temperature: 8–20°C (46–68°F).
Food: Small aquatic invertebrates, such as insects and mollusks. The fish may also accept fresh trout roe and carnivore flake.
Minimum number in the aquarium: 6.
Minimum tank size: 60 cm (24 in).
Tank region: Bottom.

Oddly, the ruffe feels "rough" to the touch. Scales are small and firmly embedded in the skin.

CENTRAL MUDMINNOW • *Umbra limi*

Size: *Males 11 cm (4.5 in), females 15 cm (6 in)*

FAMILY: UMBRIDAE (MUDMINNOWS)

Mudminnows are distant relatives of the pike – note the placement of the dorsal and anal fins. They are peaceful except during spawning, when the female is defensive of her eggs.

Origins

Quebec, in Canada, Great Lakes of the US and Ohio River

These fish can breathe through the swimbladder as well as the gills, and must be able to take in air from the surface. Their aquarium should contain soft, slightly acid water (rainwater softened over peat) and be densely planted. Provide slow but efficient filtration. Mudminnows will safely mix with like-sized tankmates, but a species tank is essential to observe their interesting spawning behavior. These fish are not readily available in some countries, but are well worth the effort.

❯ Breeding

Overwinter sexes separately in water at 5°C (40°F), continuing to feed them well. Introduce two males to one female in a tank with plenty of plants and plant debris and well-aged water. Bring the temperature slowly up to 13°C (55°F) and the fish should spawn in any available substrate material. Remove the males and allow the female to fan her 100 eggs.

Beauty in miniature

This is Umbra pygmaea, *the Eastern mudminnow, identical in size and habits to* Umbra limi *but found from Long Island south to the Neuse River, North Carolina. The species has also been introduced into Holland and parts of France. Its nearest relative is the European mudminnow,* Umbra krameri.

❯ Ideal conditions

Water: Slightly acidic, slightly soft.
Temperature: 17–21°C (62–70°F).
Food: Small aquatic insects, crayfish and mollusks and the spawn of other fish. May accept freeze-dried insect larvae.
Minimum number in the aquarium: 4.
Minimum tank size: 75 cm (30 in).
Tank region: Bottom, middle, top (to breathe).

WEATHER LOACH • *Misgurnus anguillicaudatus*

FAMILY: COBITIDAE (LOACHES)

This peaceful oddity rarely reaches its full size in the aquarium, where it spends much of the time hiding beneath rocks or bogwood. It has an elongated body, tiny eyes, and three pairs of short barbels to help it locate food. The substrate should be smooth and fine, so that these barbels are not worn down as the fish digs around for morsels. Allow plants to become well established before introducing this loach, otherwise they may be uprooted. The sexes are similar, but the second ray of the male's pelvic fin is usually thicker than that of the female.

Spawning has been reported in ponds, but not in aquariums. An albino version is also available.

Origins

Streams and rivers in the Amur region of Siberia, China, Korea, Hainan (an island in the South China Sea off the coast of southern China), and Japan.

Ideal conditions

Water: Neutral, moderately hard to hard.
Temperature: 10–15°C (50–59°F).
Food: Small live or frozen aquatic invertebrates, such as daphnia, mosquito larvae, and bloodworm. Flake foods. Some plant matter.
Minimum number in the aquarium: 2.
Minimum tank size: 60 cm (24 in).
Tank region: Bottom.

The barometer fish

The weather loach is so-called because when atmospheric pressure falls quickly, the fish becomes hyperactive and dashes around its tank. This behavior supposedly enables keepers of this fish to forecast impending thunderstorms.

This is one of the most difficult aquarium fish to catch! You'll need two nets and a lot of patience.

STONE LOACH ● *Barbatula barbatula*

FAMILY: BALITORIDAE

This is a true cold water fish, and it is difficult to keep alive if the tank temperature is allowed to rise too high. Use a powerhead or internal power filter to agitate the surface and provide a strong current. The fish is very intolerant of poor water quality.

The stone loach is not often available in aquatic outlets, but can be caught by lifting the rocks under which it lives and catching it in a hand net. Keep these peaceful fish in small groups. Males are slimmer than females and have longer pectoral fins, with a thickened second ray. Provide a smooth gravel substrate overlaid with flat stones. Suitable tankmates are gudgeon, bullheads, and minnows.

The closely related spiny loach is endangered and should not be collected. It is identifiable by a small, double-pointed spine located just below the eyes.

Ideal conditions

Water: Neutral to slightly alkaline, slightly hard.
Temperature: 10–18°C (50–64°F).
Food: Small live or frozen aquatic invertebrates, such as daphnia, tubifex (freeze-dried only), and bloodworm. Chopped earthworms. May be persuaded to take carnivore flake.
Minimum number in the aquarium: 4.
Minimum tank size: 60 cm (24 in).
Tank region: Bottom.

A dappled pattern camouflages these fish well when they venture into open water.

Breeding

The stone loach spawns between March and May. Relatively large eggs are laid onto flat stones or directly onto gravel, where they are guarded by the male. Hatching takes seven days; feed the hairlike fry on brine shrimp nauplii as a first food.
If you want to try breeding this loach, introduce two or three pairs into a species tank and condition them on live foods.

Origins
Clean, well-oxygenated streams in the UK (except Northern Scotland) and mainland Europe.

Fish for warm tanks

You can keep the species featured on pages 61–65 in a tank with water warmed to subtropical level either by a heater/thermostat or a high ambient room temperature (such as in homes with central heating). Goldfish and some fish from those featured on pages 37–59 can be mixed with these if they are all temperamentally suited, but continue to treat the tank as a cold water aquarium for stocking and planting purposes. Remember that the higher the temperature of the water, the less dissolved oxygen it can hold. On the other hand, filter bacteria will be more efficient at breaking down waste products. The warmer aquarium should be well aerated, either by a separate air pump or by the return flow from powerheads or power filters. This will ensure that the fish get all the oxygen they need. Do not be tempted to add tropical species to your slightly warmer setup. While some Asian barbs and small South American corydoras catfish will survive at a lower temperature than most community tropicals, they will not really thrive. Equally, if you warm up the aquarium to suit tropical species, you will be harming the fish described here; they will age prematurely and live for only a short time.

Right: The Li River near Guilin, China. The country that pioneered goldfish culture is also home to several fish species that prefer a slightly warm tank.

WHITE CLOUD MOUNTAIN MINNOW ● *Tanichthys albonubes*

FAMILY: CYPRINIDAE

White Clouds are a useful addition to the setup, being inexpensive and attractive schoolers, very tolerant of low temperatures, and easy to spawn. They have been known to survive winters outdoors in iced-over water casks!

Males are slimmer and more colorful than females; the stripe down the sides looks iridescent under aquarium lights, justifying the nickname "poor man's neon tetra." White Clouds will show their best colors if fed live foods.

A long-finned variety is available; if you choose these fish, do not mix them with fin-nippers. Originating from cool, well-oxygenated waters, White Clouds require strong but not turbulent filtration and a well-furnished aquarium with dense cover from fine-leaved plants.

▷ Breeding

Condition your breeding stock on plenty of live foods, and in the late evening introduce a pair into a separate spawning tank three-quarters filled. This should contain only a sponge filter, a nylon spawning mop, and a substrate of marbles or artificial spawning grass. Top off the tank with cold water that has been allowed to stand for 24 hours. The pair should spawn early the following morning, scattering their eggs. Some will adhere to the mop, others will fall into crevices in the substrate, where the parents cannot reach them. Remove the adults when spawning is complete. Tiny transparent fry will hatch in three to four days. Provide infusoria or a liquid preparation for baby egglayers as their first foods.

Origins

Streams and rivers on the White Cloud Mountain, near Canton, southern China.

This is the elegant long-finned form of the White Cloud Mountain minnow.

▷ Ideal conditions

Water: Neutral, slightly soft to slightly hard.
Temperature: 18–22°C (64–72°F).
Food: Flake, small live foods, freeze-dried or frozen daphnia, bloodworm, and mosquito larvae.
Minimum number in the aquarium: 6.
Minimum tank size: 60 cm (24 in).
Tank region: Middle to top.

WESTERN MOSQUITOFISH • *Gambusia affinis*

FAMILY: POECILIIDAE (LIVEBEARING TOOTHCARPS)

The western mosquitofish is one of only two livebearing species featured in this book. Its common name is well-deserved, as it has been introduced all over the world to control malarial mosquitoes. The species flourishes in most situations, as it is tolerant of high temperatures, low levels of dissolved oxygen, and even some salinity – it will survive in tidal rivers well down into estuaries. Stock at least three females to every male, otherwise the male will chase and stress tankmates with a constant pressure to mate.

The gonopodium (organ of reproduction) is carried flat to the body when not being deployed by this male G. affinis holbrooki.

Breeding

Males use a modified anal fin (gonopodium) to fertilize females internally. After a four-week gestation period, when the female will develop a dark "gravid spot," she gives birth to up to 50 fully formed fry. In a densely planted species tank, some may survive to a size where the parents no longer eat them, but for best results rear them separately.

Ideal conditions

Water: Slightly acidic to slightly alkaline, hard.
Temperature: 18–24°C (64–75°F).
Food: Will eat flake and frozen food, but relishes small live foods, such as daphnia, cyclops, and midge/mosquito larvae.
Minimum number in the aquarium: 4 (1 male, 3 females).
Minimum tank size: 45 cm (18 in).
Tank region: Middle to top.

Right: Female mosquitofish are larger than males, and easy to tell apart by their unmodified anal fin and plumper body profile.

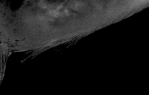

Origins

Originally from Texas and the western US, now widespread in southern Europe, inland along the Mediterranean coast.

DWARF TOPMINNOW • *Heterandria formosa*

FAMILY: POECILIIDAE (LIVEBEARING TOOTHCARPS)

Beauty can definitely arrive in small packages, as these are among the world's tiniest backboned animals. Do not, therefore, mix them with other fish, however "non-predatory" these may seem. A densely planted species aquarium will suit them better, allowing them to reproduce undisturbed and with a high percentage of fry survival.

These fish are farmed for the aquarium trade, so buy only well-quarantined stock and try to match your aquarium water chemistry to that of your dealer's. Later on, you may adjust it gradually to the ideal, if necessary.

The male dwarf topminnow rivals some marine gobies for the title of the "world's smallest fish."

By bringing live young and not eggs into the world, female livebearers have increased the odds of survival many times over.

Origin

South Carolina

Ideal conditions

Water: Neutral, moderately hard.
Temperature: 17–26°C (62–79°F).
Food: Relishes small live aquatic invertebrates, but will also take flake and freeze-dried larvae.
Minimum number in the aquarium: 4 (1 male, 3 females).
Minimum tank size: 45 cm (18 in).
Tank region: Middle to top.

Breeding

The gestation period of these prolific livebearers is just two weeks. Supply them with fine-leaved plants, including floating species, such as *Riccia fluitans*, amongst which the newly born fry may hide. Or float practice golf balls on the surface to provide a refuge. Stock in the ratio one male to three females.

MEDAKA • *Oryzias latipes*

FAMILY: ORIZYIATIDAE (RICEFISH)

Rice paddies are the adopted home of these efficient little predators of mosquito larvae. There are several color morphs, the most common being white and orange. Males have more silvery scales to the rear of the body than females. They are slimmer, and the anal fin is larger and pointed.

Because of their small size, keep medakas either in a species aquarium or in the company of other fish that will not view them as a handy snack! Give them a well-planted tank with gentle, but efficient, filtration that fully circulates the water.

Origins

China, Japan, South Korea.

When wild fish are brightly colored, it is for a reason – sometimes for courtship, sometimes to signal that they are well capable of defending themselves. The medaka matches perfectly the yellow mud of its native rivers, against which a darker fish would stand out and be vulnerable to predators.

▶ Ideal conditions

Water: Neutral, slightly soft to moderately hard.
Temperature: 18–23°C (64–73°F).
Food: Small live or frozen aquatic invertebrates, flake.
Minimum number in the aquarium: 4.
Minimum tank size: 45 cm (18 in).
Tank region: Middle to top.

▶ Breeding

Medakas breed in a unique way. The females release a modest cluster of large, amber-colored eggs, which remain attached to the area of the vent. After fertilization, they are wiped off onto plants. This technique is not as efficient as that of the livebearers, but ensures a better fry survival rate than can be expected with casual egg-scatterers.

MANCHURIAN TIGER LOACH • *Leptobotia mantschurica*

FAMILY: COBITIDAE (LOACHES)

This attractive loach with distinctive, narrow striping is not the easiest fish to maintain. It likes a large, roomy tank with a sandy or very fine gravel substrate, hiding places (rocks and/or bogwood), good aeration, but not too much turbulence.

The sexes are similar, but the males have a divided spine below the eye. This fish can be kept with others of similar size, but some individuals are quite aggressive. You will need to watch a new introduction to make sure it does not bully its tankmates. Breeding is unlikely in the aquarium.

Origins

Asia, Russia, and China. Amur basin, Ussuri and Sungari basins, Liao He River.

"Tiger" by name and sometimes by nature, this loach can be rather secretive.

Ideal conditions

Water: Neutral, slightly soft to slightly hard.
Temperature: 10–20°C (50–68°F).
Food: Prefers small live foods, but will take frozen or freeze-dried mosquito larvae, daphnia, and sometimes flake.
Minimum number in the aquarium: 1.
Minimum tank size: 75 cm (30 in).
Tank region: Bottom.

Fish for large tanks

All the fish mentioned up to now will benefit from a tank larger than the specified minimum size. But in the case of the species featured on pages 67–75, spacious accommodation is essential! Do not even consider buying these fish unless you can provide an aquarium measuring at least 180x60x60 cm (72x24x24 in) with a capacity of 150 gallons (454 liters). Bear in mind the space this will take up, its filled weight (over 450 kg / nearly 1000 lbs), and the extra initial and ongoing costs of filtration, lighting, and aeration. While some of these larger fish are gregarious vegetarians, others are out-and-out predators and will need a tank to themselves. Piscivores naturally feed on other, live fish, but the examples chosen can all be persuaded to accept dead fish and meat items.

Big fish generate a great deal of potentially harmful bodily waste, so filters must be up to the task. Some fishkeepers run large cold water tanks on pond-sized "black box" filters or build their own multichambered filters that sit alongside or beneath the tank. Keeping big fish is a true enthusiast's hobby.

Right: Florida is home to some of the world's largest freshwater fish. Beneath the tranquil waters of St. Marks National Wildlife Reserve could lurk tank-busting alligator gars!

GRASS CARP, WHITE AMUR • *Ctenopharyngodon idella*

FAMILY: CYPRINIDAE

Grass carp are primarily pond fish, but smaller specimens may be kept indoors. The natural coloration of these streamlined creatures is silvery gray, but albinos are available through pet stores. (However, some southern US states prohibit the keeping of this species.) Although commonly known as a grass carp, it prefers commercial pond pellets to natural green food and cannot be relied upon to keep its tank free of algae. It will, however, eat or uproot all known aquarium plants, so restrict the decor to artificial plants, along with rockwork and bogwood. Provide heavy filtration.

Ideal conditions

Water: Neutral, moderately hard to hard.
Temperature: 10–20°C (50–68°F).
Food: Fresh lettuce, cucumber, zucchini; wheat germ-based pond pellets.
Minimum number in the aquarium: 2.
Minimum tank size:
180 cm (72 in).
Tank region:
Middle to top.

Origins

Amur River and lowland rivers of China, but widely introduced elsewhere for weed clearance.

Breeding

Grass carp will survive in water down to 10°C (50°F), but need much higher temperatures (26°C/79°F) before they will spawn. The eggs are semi-buoyant, and after fertilization they are washed downstream to quieter reaches of the river, where they hatch. Aquarium spawnings are unlikely, given the size of mature adults.

As grass carp are agile and skittish, keep the tank covered at all times, otherwise the fish will end up on the floor.

Grass carp are identifiable by the eyes, level with the jawline.

KOI ● *Cyprinus carpio*

FAMILY: CYPRINIDAE

Koi, or nishikigoi, are simply ornamental varieties of the common carp, a fish that has been introduced to Europe, Australia, and the US and is kept by aquarists worldwide. Koi are farmed in Israel, Japan, and the US – anywhere the climate is warm enough to promote rapid growth.

It is fun to buy half a dozen young (15 cm/6 in) fish and rear them indoors in a slightly warm aquarium, where a growth rate of 10 cm/4 in a year is attainable. This allows you to view the koi from the side, something that is not possible in ponds.

Koi have a reputation for destroying plants, so keep them in a tank furnished with bogwood and/or smooth rocks, plus plastic plants siliconed to sheets of slate buried in a medium gravel substrate. Change at least 20% of the water each week and provide heavy aeration.

Koi are messy feeders. To keep the water clear and clean, combine internal and external power filtration, or run the tank on undergravel filters with powerheads. Fit heavy lids on the aquarium, as koi are great jumpers. You can safely mix them with fancy goldfish.

Origins

Eastern Asia (Black, Azof, Caspian, and Aral Seas) and China.

You can feed koi kept indoors all year round, and growth is astonishing. Move them to your pond when they outgrow the aquarium.

► Ideal conditions

Water: Neutral, moderately hard.
Temperature: 10–24°C (50–75°F).
Food: Floating and sinking koi pellets, pondsticks, fresh orange and lettuce, prawns, earthworms.
Minimum number in the aquarium: 3.
Minimum tank size: 180 cm (72 in).
Tank region: Top, middle, and bottom.

Left: This is a Shusui koi, a German-scaled (Doitsu) version of one of the first koi varieties to be developed, the Asagi. Doitsu koi, with their reflective scales, look good in a side-lit aquarium.

Keeping koi in a pond

Koi ponds differ from goldfish ponds in needing constant, quality filtration and a minimum depth of 120 cm (4 ft). Plants are rarely included, but the fish themselves provide all the color you could wish for. In good conditions, koi can grow to 1 m (39 in).

Right: There are about 13 judging varieties of koi. This is a young Hikari Utsuri – a metallic Showa – actually a black fish with gold markings and not the other way around.

BARBEL ● *Barbus barbus*

FAMILY: CYPRINIDAE

Barbel favor clean, briskly flowing rivers, where they hug the gravel bottom against the current. Keep their aquarium cool at all times and furnish it with smooth rocks and a substrate of medium gravel. Heavy filtration and powerful aeration are essential.

The fish gets its common name from the two pairs of prominent, fleshy barbels used to locate food. Young specimens resemble gudgeon, but are less colorful, more streamlined, and very muscular, with small scales. Albino and steel-blue barbel are now available in limited numbers.

Aquarium breeding is not practical; in the wild, barbel spawn in early summer on gravel shallows.

Ideal conditions

Water: Neutral, slightly soft to moderately hard.
Temperature: 10–15°C (50–59°F).
Food: Meaty frozen foods, freeze-dried krill, live crayfish. Will also take flake and sinking pond pellets.
Minimum number in the aquarium: 2.
Minimum tank size: 180 cm (72 in).
Tank region: Bottom (but learns to feed from the surface).

Barbel thrive in an aquarium with strong currents provided by powerheads or return flows from an external canister filter.

Origins

Clean rivers in the UK and mainland Europe, where related species are found. Introduced as a sport fish to British stillwaters and rivers where they do not naturally occur.

These whiskers (also known as barbels) are laden with sensors for locating food items.

BOWFIN ● *Amia calva*

FAMILY: AMIIDAE

This is an oddball, a relic of Jurassic times, with a skeleton made up largely of cartilage. It shares another sharklike characteristic; its teeth are retractable.

In the wild, it is found in sluggish creeks and bayous, which are often oxygen-deficient. It has adapted to these conditions by being able to breathe surface air.

Youngsters of both sexes have caudal ocelli (black spots ringed with pale gold), but the females lose the outer ring as they mature.

Young specimens may be kept with spotted gar of similar size, but as they grow they become exclusively piscivorous and are best kept alone or only as compatible pairs. They are intelligent fish with real character and soon learn to recognize their owner. Provide excellent filtration and plenty of retreats in the form of plant thickets and bogwood.

Cool customers

Bowfins from the northern end of their range require a cold winter period (below 10°C/50°F), otherwise they may not feed well for the rest of the year.

Origins

Drainages of the Mississippi River and Lakes Erie and Huron, eastern US.

▶ Breeding

When the water temperature reaches 22°C (72°F), the male chews down a patch of marginal water plants in a sheltered spot to form a nest up to 60 cm (24 in) across. Into this he lures a succession of females, who each lay up to 10,000 large green adhesive eggs. These are fanned for up to six days until they hatch, when the father escorts a large cloud of fry in search of small aquatic insects and hovers beneath them while they feed. Aquarium spawnings have not been recorded but would seem quite feasible, given the necessary space!

▶ Ideal conditions

Water: Slightly acidic, slightly soft.
Temperature: 10–22°C (50–72°F).
Food: Offer young fish shrimp, crayfish, meaty frozen foods, and carnivore pellets. Young adults can be trained to accept dead trout. Avoid fatty items.
Minimum number in the aquarium: 1.
Minimum tank size: 215 cm (84 in) and proportionately deep.
Tank region: Bottom, middle, and top.

Appealing bowfin youngsters such as this should not be bought unless you can house them into adulthood.

PIKE ● *Esox lucius*

Size: *Males to 60 cm (24 in), females 150 cm (60 in) or larger*

FAMILY: ESOCIDAE

These voracious lurking predators relish aquatic insects and their own siblings when young, moving on to other fish species, rats, and water birds as they grow. In the UK, the largest specimens are found in trout reservoirs, where they find easy pickings!

Juveniles have vertical camouflage striping, which changes to a dappled pattern as they mature. The pretty youngsters are both more practical and attractive to keep than adult pike, which are highly sedentary unless in feeding mode. One per tank is the safe option; there need be only a tiny difference in size before one young pike attempts to swallow another. This sometimes results in the death of both, as the aggressor bites off more than it can chew.

Spawning takes place in early spring, when the water is still very cold. Several small males (jacks) follow the "mother ship" female into plant thickets in the shallows.

Provide an aquarium with gentle but efficient filtration and do not allow it to get too warm. Supply rock and bogwood hideouts. Small pike will take live minnows (which they kill instantly). It is better to train them to take pieces of trout or other oily fish, such as herring and mackerel.

A smart young prototype of a pike in typical striped juvenile pattern. No two individuals are marked the same.

Below: *The chain pickerel (Esox niger) is an American native fish. This subadult shows the markings that give it its common name.*

Origins

Lakes and slow-moving rivers in the UK, mainland Europe, and eastern US (where it is known as the northern pike).

Ideal conditions

Water: Neutral, slightly soft to slightly hard.
Temperature: 10–24°C (50–75°F).
Food: In the wild, young pike take fish fry and aquatic invertebrates, moving on to a largely piscivorous diet, with mammals and aquatic birds if found. In the aquarium, offer dead fish.
Maximum number in the aquarium: 1.
Minimum tank size: 180 cm (72 in).
Tank region: Bottom, middle, and top.

SPOTTED GAR • *Lepisosteus oculatus*

FAMILY: LEPISOSTEIDAE

Gars are ancient fish with hard, enamelled "ganoid" scales that form a flexible suit of armor. They are not closely related to pike, but the arrangement of the dorsal and anal fins far back toward the tail enables them to achieve great speed from a standing start and maintain it just long enough to seize their prey. The shortnosed gar *(Lepisosteus platostomus,* not shown here) grows to a length of 60 cm (24 in) – a more manageable size than its relatives. In all gars, the slim jaws are equipped with fine, backward-pointing teeth.

A juvenile spotted gar. A heavy tank cover will prevent this strong fish from jumping out and ending up on the floor.

Left: *One for the true enthusiast, the alligator gar* (Lepiosteus tristoechus) *grows to 300 cm (118 in).*

Origins

Great Lakes, Mississippi drainage, and down the Gulf Coast to western Florida.

▶ Ideal conditions

Water: Neutral, slightly to moderately hard.
Temperature: 12–18°C (53–64°F).
Food: Exclusively fish when juvenile/adult, but with perseverance can be persuaded to take dead prey.
Minimum number in the aquarium: 1.
Minimum tank size: 210 cm (84 in).
Tank region: Middle and top.

PERCH • *Perca fluviatilis*

FAMILY: PERCIDAE (PERCHES)

Young specimens look their best when kept in schools, but as they grow they become more solitary. Perch (the European equivalent of the US's freshwater bass/sunfish) are well-known to anglers, as they take any lively bait readily and greedily.

Their striped camouflage coloration is a clue to their lifestyle, as they congregate in plant thickets in shaded cover, typically under bridges or overhanging trees, occasionally "pack ambushing" schools of minnows, which panic and scatter on the surface.

Perch are not particularly aggressive to other fish species of comparable size, but they require a large, well-planted aquarium, ideally with bogwood structures rising to just below the surface.

This slim youngster will become much deeper-bodied as it grows. Note the spiny first dorsal fin, which makes life hard for would-be predators.

Origins

The UK and mainland Europe, eastwards to Siberia and south to the Pyrenees.

Ideal conditions

Water: Neutral, slightly hard.
Temperature: 8–20°C (46–68°F).
Food: Aquatic invertebrates, worms and, later, smaller fish. In the aquarium they can be persuaded to take carnivore flake and small dead prey, such as whitebait and lancefish.
Minimum number in the aquarium: 4.
Minimum tank size: 180 cm (72 in).
Tank region: Bottom, middle, and top.

Breeding

The fish spawn in spring, in plant thickets in the shallows. Lacy strings of adhesive eggs are wrapped around plants and willow roots. Aquarium spawnings are rare but feasible, although the parents must be removed after spawning, otherwise they will consume the eggs and fry.

SAILFIN SUCKER ● *Myxocyprinus asiaticus*

FAMILY: CATOSTOMIDAE

With their deep, laterally compressed bodies, brown-and-cream barring extending into the fins, and sail-like dorsals, young specimens are a very tempting buy. However, as they grow (which they do very quickly), the coloration becomes quite drab and the barring fades.

These are quite peaceful fish, but can be nervous, dashing around the aquarium and injuring themselves on sharp rocks. Restrict the decor to rounded pebbles and then the fish can graze on algae. Filtration needs to be of the highest standard, and these fish appreciate some current in the tank.

Captive breeding has not been observed, possibly because mature specimens require so much space.

Origins

Cool, fast to medium-paced streams and rivers in Asia and northern China.

The sail-like dorsal may be used as a stabilizing fin as the fish works its way upstream.

The camouflage mottling of this youngster is not needed when the fish attains adulthood, and duly fades.

Ideal conditions

Water: Neutral, slightly hard.
Temperature: 15–28°C (59–82°F).
Food: Flake, frozen and freeze-dried meaty foods, algae wafers.
Minimum number in the aquarium: 2.
Minimum tank size: 180 cm (72 in), less for juveniles.
Tank region: Bottom and middle.

INDEX

Page numbers in **bold** indicate major entries; *italics* refer to captions and annotations; plain type indicates other text entries.

CREDITS

The practical photographs featured in this book have been taken by Geoffrey Rogers and are © Interpet Publishing.

The publishers would like to thank the following photographers for providing images, credited here by page number and position: B(Bottom), T(Top), C(Center), BL(Bottom Left), etc.

Heather Angel/Natural Visions: 11, 60
MP & C Piednoir/Aqua Press: Title page, 6, 13, 28(L), 55, 72(T)
Dave Bevan: Contents page (L), 16(BL,BR), 23(B), 26, 34(R), 44, 45(B), 46, 62(B), 64, 69(TL,BR)
John Feltwell/Wildlife Matters: 36
Frank Lane Picture Agency: 37, 38, 40(TR), 66(Leo Batten)
Arend van den Nieuwenhuizen: 22(R), 24(L), 42(T), 62(T)
Aaron Norman: Contents page (TR), 9(T), 22(L), 27(L), 29(L), 31(TR), 33, 34(L), 41, 43(T), 47, 48, 49(L,R), 50, 52, 53(T), 57(T), 57(B), 61(B), 71, 72(B)
Photomax (Max Gibbs): 9(B), 17, 18, 19, 21(B), 23(T), 24(T), 25(B,TR), 28(R), 29(R), 30(L), 31(B), 32(L), 35, 39, 42(B), 43(B), 51, 54, 58, 59, 61(T), 63, 65, 67, 68, 70, 73(T), 74
Fred Rosenzweig: 39(R), 32(R)
Mike Sandford: 8(B), 12, 40(B), 45(TR), 53(B), 56, 73(B)
W A Tomey: Copyright page, 20, 27(R), 75

The artwork illustrations have been prepared by Stuart Watkinson and are © Interpet Publishing.

The publishers would like to thank Kerry and Andrew at Heaver Tropics, Ash, Kent and Drew Simons at The Koi Waterlife Centre, Southfleet, Kent for their help during the preparation of this book.

The information and recommendations in this book are given without any guarantees on the part of the author and publisher, who disclaim any liability with the use of this material.